NO EMPTY PHRASES

To Ann

critic and encourager

When you are praying, do not heap up empty phrases...
Matthew 6. 7a, NRSV

If ever, Lord, we meet to praise your name,
sanctuary-safe within the hallowed walls,
and try by prayer, or hymn,
by solemn silence or full-throated praise
   to close the doors and keep the world at bay,
   to shade the windows lest the light distracts,
   ignore the sounds of traffic, passing feet, bird-song or voice,
then, Lord, rebuke us,
and fresh remind us of your loving care for all that you have made:
   its nature: cruel and kind; its people: sinners, saints;
   and of a cross, up-reared to save them all.
Then call us back, to worship you aright, in spirit and in truth.

from *The Word in the World*, NCEC

NO EMPTY PHRASES

An anthology of poetry and prose for
Christian education and worship
based on the Lord's Prayer

Compiled by

Donald Hilton

NCEC

Cover design by Peggy Chapman

Published by:
National Christian Education Council
1020 Bristol Road
Selly Oak
Birmingham
B29 6LB

British Library Cataloguing-in-Publication Data:
A catalogue record for this book is available from the British Library.

ISBN 0–7197–0947–4

First published 1999

Typeset by National Christian Education Council
Printed and bound in Great Britain by
Biddles Ltd, Guildford and King's Lynn

Contents

Various versions of the Lord's Prayer appear on pages 2, 14, 26, 64, 86, 118, 134, 166, 178, 196 and 210.

Preface

The Lord's Prayer is older than the Church. Matthew (6.9ff) suggests that it was given spontaneously by Jesus. This account sets the prayer in the context of wider teaching about prayer and prefaces it with a particular desire to avoid 'vain repetition', 'babbling' or 'empty phrases'. Luke (11.1ff) gives the initiative to the disciples who, knowing that John the Baptist had taught his disciples to pray, sought the same help from Jesus. Again, the context is not without significance: Luke prefaces the gift of the prayer with a story about Mary's quiet acceptance of Jesus' presence as against Martha's busyness, and follows it with the parable of the friend who came at midnight to seek help and was commended by the story-teller for his persistence.

Each account makes it clear that the prayer in some form had its origin in the ministry of Jesus. It is not surprising, therefore, that it has been held in high regard by Christians throughout two millennia and stands central in Christian worship today. In addition to its use in private devotion, it has been used in all the historic liturgies since about 400AD.

However, it is realistic rather than merely provocative to say that there is no such thing as 'The Lord's Prayer' if by that we mean a precise set of agreed words universally used by Christians from the time of Jesus. Different versions are in evidence from the biblical records themselves. Whilst the essential meaning is constant, the versions in the Gospels of Matthew and Luke vary significantly. Further, marginal notes in Bibles show that there are many variations in the available manuscripts of both Gospels. Manuscripts of Matthew show four variants, whilst Luke has no less than six. A version close to Matthew's is included in the *Didache,* an early manual of Christian morals and Church practice, which recommended the use of the prayer three times a day. As early as the third century, Cyprian was offering a personal interpretation of 'daily bread' as the bread of Holy Communion.

To show the variety the prayer enjoys and also the way that translators have struggled with the meaning of several of the phrases in the prayer, each section of the anthology is prefaced with a different version. Such variety of text and interpretation should not surprise us. It is a living prayer. It was offered as a guide or model, not as a prescribed text from which there should be no variation, and its influence and universal relevance may well lie in its elusiveness.

This anthology begins with items which show that our own generation is continuing the process of using the prayer as a model. It is the hope of the compiler that throughout the book the imagination of those who use it will be stirred so that the relevance of the prayer will be discovered alike in daily life and in the sanctuary.

Donald Hilton
Ashby St. Mary, Norwich
August 1999

Pray in this way...

The Lord's Prayer was given to us to help us avoid 'vain repetition'. It was offered as a guide or model and not as a prescribed text from which there should be no variation. It is, therefore, a living prayer capable of re-interpretation and fresh expression in every generation. It is not surprising, therefore, that so many variations of the prayer appear in the manuscripts of the New Testament as local groups of early Christians emphasized different elements of the prayer in order to express their own deep convictions and longings.

The process has continued. Taking the biblical texts as starting points, Christians in our own generation have continued to *pray in this way...*

Versions of the Lord's Prayer

The English Language Liturgical Commission version

This is approved world-wide in English speaking Churches. It is commended by the Anglican Communion, many Reformed Churches, the Roman Catholic Church, but not the Orthodox Church. It is the version from which the section headings of this anthology are drawn.

Our Father in heaven,
hallowed be your name,
your kingdom come,
your will be done on earth as in heaven.
Give us today our daily bread.
Forgive us our sins
as we forgive those who sin against us.
Save us from the time of trial
and deliver us from evil.
For the kingdom, the power and the glory are yours
now and for ever. Amen

Pray in this way...

1

Dearest Father who lives in heaven,
may your name be kept pure.
Let peace reign and everyone be equal
on earth as in heaven.
Provide us with our daily needs as well as our spiritual needs.
Please forgive us the things we have done wrong
as we will forget the bad things others have done to us.
Help us not to be tempted to hurt you
and keep Satan away from us.
Because you made the earth and heaven and everything in it
and you are all powerful and we should give you glory
through all eternity.
We all agree with this!

from North India
written at a children's camp

2

Our Father
who is here on earth
holy is your name
in the hungry who share their bread and their song.
Your kingdom come,
a generous land where confidence and truth reign.
Let us do your will
being a cool breeze for those who sweat.
You are giving us our daily bread
when we manage to get back our lands
or to get a fairer wage.
Forgive us
for keeping silent in the face of injustice
and for burying our dreams.
Don't let us fall into the temptation
of taking up the same arms as the enemy,
but deliver us from evil which disunites us.
And we shall have believed in humanity and in life
and we shall have known your kingdom
which is being built for ever and ever

from Central America
(a shortened version)

Pray in this way...

3
Eternal God
We say good morning to you.
Hallowed be your name.
Early in the morning, before we begin our work
we praise your glory.
Renew our bodies as fresh as the morning flowers.
Open our inner eyes, as the sun casts new light upon the darkness
which prevailed over the night.
Deliver us from all captivity.
Give us wings of freedom, like the birds in the sky,
to begin a new journey.
Restore justice and freedom as a mighty stream
running continuously as day follows day.
We thank you for the gift of this morning,
and a new day to work with you.

Masao Takenaka, Japan

4
Our Father, who are in this our land,
    may your name be blessed
in our incessant search for justice and peace.
    May your kingdom come
for those who have for centuries awaited a life of dignity.
    May your will be done on earth and in heaven
and in the church of Central America,
    a church on the side of the poor.
Give us today our daily bread to build a new society.
    Forgive us our trespasses,
do not let us fall into the temptation
    of believing ourselves already new men and women.
And deliver us from the evil of war
    and from the evil of forgetting that our lives
and the life of this country are in your hands.

from Nicaragua

5

Eternal Spirit,
Life-Giver, Pain-Bearer, Love-Maker,
Source of all that is and that shall be,
Father and Mother of us all,
Loving God, in whom is heaven:

The Hallowing of your Name
    echo through the universe!
The Way of your Justice
    be followed by the peoples of the world!
Your Heavenly Will
    be done by all created beings!
Your Commonwealth of Peace and Freedom
    sustain our hope and come on earth!

With the bread we need for today,
    feed us.
In the hurts we absorb from one another,
    forgive us.
In times of temptation and test,
    strengthen us.
From trials too great to endure,
    spare us.
From the grip of all that is evil,
    free us.

For you reign in the glory
of the power that is love,
now and for ever. Amen

Jim Cotter

Pray in this way...

6   *Praying with Christ*
Dear God,
our Creator,
Beloved Companion
and Guide upon the Way,
Eternal Spirit
within us
and beyond us...

Let us honour
your name
in lives of costly,
giving love...

Let us show that we
and all whom we meet
deserve dignity and respect,
for they are your dwelling place
and your home...

Let us share in action
your deep desire
for justice and peace
among the peoples
of the world...

Let us share our bread
with one another,
the bread that you have shared
with us...

Let us in the spirit
of your forgiving us,
make friends
with those we have harmed
and failed to love...

Let us overcome
our trials and temptations,
our suffering and courage
with which you overcame them too...

Let us in your love
free the world from evil,
transforming darkness into light...

For the whole universe is yours,
and you invite us to be partners
in the work of your creating...

Amen. So be it.
So will we do it.

Jim Cotter

7

Eternal Spirit of the universe:
 Father who continuously begets creation,
 Mother who constantly nurtures life,
You are worthy of all praise!

You are holy beyond our understanding and reach,
 yet you touch us into life.
You live in the eternal beyond,
 yet you dwell in every passing moment.

May your loving purpose come to fruition
alike in the highest heaven
and the breadth of the earth.

Unless you forgive us, we are lost
but your loving-kindness is unshakeable
and your compassion unlocks our forgiveness
for those who wrong us.

Give us strength always to be faithful to you
in things great
and small.
Release us
 from the grip of evil in ourselves.
Deliver us
 from the hurt that others would inflict on us.
Liberate our common life
 from all that distorts community or hinders justice

For everything is yours
 in heaven and on earth!
You are revealed alike
 in power and glory,
 in vulnerability and humility.
You have been the same from the beginning,
and remain the same beyond eternity.

Donald Hilton

8

Great Eternal One
Creator of the universe
holy is your name;
your kingdom stretches across the face
of the earth, embracing us all.

Glory and power are yours forever.

We seek to know your will —
help us.
We seek to do your will —
guide us.

The fruits of the earth come from your hand;
we thank you for your mercy.
We are surrounded by your compassion and love;
your generosity knows no end.
Give us your grace to be generous to others.
You forgive us when we fail you;
help us to forgive each other,
and to bring in your kingdom
of justice and love
that all people may sing of your power
and your glory forever and forever.

Alison O'Grady

9   *Caribbean Lord's Prayer*

Our Father who is in heaven
Hallowed be Your Name,
Your Kingdom come, Your will be done,
Hallowed be Your Name.

On earth as it is in heaven,
Hallowed be Your Name,
Give us this day our daily bread,
Hallowed be Your Name.

Forgive us all our trespasses,
Hallowed be Your Name,
As we forgive those who trespass against us,
Hallowed be Your Name.

And lead us not into temptation,
Hallowed be Your Name,
But deliver us from all that is evil,
Hallowed be Your Name.

For Yours is the Kingdom, the Power and the Glory
Hallowed be Your Name,
For ever and for ever and ever,
Hallowed be Your Name.

Amen, Amen, it shall be so,
Hallowed be Your Name,
Amen, Amen, it shall be so,
Hallowed be Your name.

From the Caribbean

10   *A Dialogue on the Lord's Prayer*

Lord, as you told us, so we pray
For others, folk in need.

> You left a model for our prayers.
> We have it off by heart.
> But have we understood it?

We intercede, we ask your help
That all these things may happen:
The sick be healed, the hungry fed, the poor relieved.

> But are these the things we truly want
> Within our hearts
> And nothing for ourselves?
> Truly, nothing?

We aren't poor and hungry,
We've got doctors when we're ill;
We're doing very nicely, thank you.
But these folk really need your help.

> Read the prayer again.
> Give *us*, lead *us*, forgive *us* —
> The word is always *us*
> Except 'those trespassers',
> The ones who separate themselves
> And their possessions
> from the needs of others.
> Those who do not share
> Resources, money, food.

Lord, are we 'us' or 'them'?
Can you see any difference?

> Lord, by the times we have known the goodness of food
> and by the times we have known hunger
> give your children bread
> or rice, or cassava.

Give your brothers food.
But we don't know how to do it;
We are afraid to do it,
For all of us are caught up
In the power of the systems of this world.
Help us, Lord. All of us.

Lord, by the abundance of our possessions,
and any poverty we may have known
we pray for all who are enslaved
by poverty of riches
in a system that reckons worth by possessions.

Help us to see ourselves
and to value ourselves
not as the world does
but by the way you see us
and value us
rich and poor alike.

Lord, by our health and by our sickness,
by the suffering we have known
and by our fear of it,
we pray for all who suffer
whatever the nature of their suffering may be
whether it shows or not.

In suffering there is no 'us' and no 'them'
But each of us is joined and at one
As Jesus suffered
In whose name
We offer these our prayers to You.

W. S. Beattie

Pray in this way...

11 *Praying in Christ*

Abba, Amma, Beloved...
your name be hallowed...
your reign spread among us...
your will be done well...
at all times, in all places...
on earth, as in heaven...

Give us the bread...
we need for today...
Forgive us the trespass...
as we forgive those...
who trespass against us...
Let us not fail...
in time of our testing...
Spare us from trials...
too sharp to endure...
Free us from the grip...
of all evil powers...

For yours is the reign...
the power and the glory...
the victory of love...
for time and eternity...
world without end...
So be it. Amen...

Jim Cotter

Our Father in heaven

...having a thousand names and none —

Versions of the Lord's Prayer

The traditional version

Our Father, which art in heaven,
hallowed be thy name;
thy kingdom come;
thy will be done in earth as it is in heaven.
Give us this day our daily bread,
and forgive us our trespasses
as we forgive them that trespass against us,
and lead us not into temptation
but deliver us from evil.
For thine is the kingdom, the power and the glory
for ever and ever. Amen

12 *A prayer of longing and letting go*

You for whom I wait,
unknown, unheard, invisible —
having a thousand names and none —
reach towards me
as I reach out for you;
and be known in the encounter,
heard in the stillness,
seen in the mist and the darkness,
and named fleetingly.
And then
enable me to let go again
of the knowing
the hearing
the glimpsing
and the naming —
content to be poor in spirit
and to travel light,
emptied of all desire
to bind, restrain or define you,
seeking always
to be attentive to you
in the present moment
where you are lively
and new
and always
surprising.

Kate Compston

13 *Names without number*

God is hidden, no one knows his form,
No one has searched out his similitude.
God is hidden to gods and men.
He is secret to all creatures.
No one knows a name by which to call him.
His name is hidden.
His name is a secret to all his children.
His names are without number.
His names are many; no one knows the number thereof.

Old Egyptian

14 *After Communion*

Why should I call Thee Lord, Who art my God?
  Why should I call Thee Friend, Who art my Love?
Or King, Who art my very Spouse above?
Or call Thy Sceptre on my heart Thy rod?
  Lo now Thy banner over me is love,
All heaven flies open to me at Thy nod:
For Thou hast lit Thy flame in me a clod,
  Made me a nest for dwelling of Thy Dove.
  What wilt Thou call me in our home above,
Who now hast called me friend? How will it be
  When Thou for good wine settest forth Thy best?
Now Thou dost bid me come and sup with Thee,
  Now Thou dost make me lean upon Thy breast:
How will it be with me in time of love?

Christina Rossetti

15 *In the Beginning*

God laughed,
And the firmament fumed and spluttered with pleasure;
And the sea shook the foam of his hair from his eyes;
And earth was glad.

The sound of laughter
Was like the swaying and swinging of thunder in mirth;
Like the rush of the north on a drowsy and dozing land;
It was cool. It was clear.

The lion leapt down
At the bleating of the frightened lamb and smiled;
And the viper was tamed by the thrill of the earth,
At the holy laughter.

We laughed,
For the Lord was laughing with us in the evening;
The laughter of love went pealing into the night:
And it was good.

Paul Bunday

16 *Mother me, my Father*

Mother me, my Father,
That I may step unbowed
From safe within your haven
To face a hostile crowd.

Mother me, my Father,
And help to ease the pain
Of taunts and tears and teasing
And make me love again.

Mother me, my Father,
With hands so deeply scarred,
That I may touch some other
Whose suffering is hard.

Mother me, my Father,
That all my life be styled
On loving like a mother
And trusting like a child.

Helena McKinnon

17 *A labour of love*

Once upon a time,
in the beginning,
a labour of love was undertaken.

It started with a sign,
to show that something was about to happen.
Light came forth from the deep darkness,
bright, clear and unmistakable.

And it was very good.

At the second time,
the waters were broken.
At first, they gushed,
then they dried to a trickle,
And a space was created.
It was exactly the right size.
By now, creation was well under way.

And it was very good.

At the third time,
a cradle was made ready.
It was comfortable and beautiful and waiting.
And food was prepared,
issuing warmly and sweetly
and in precisely the right measure
from the being of the labourer.

And it was very good.

At the fourth time,
rhythm was established.
Ebbing and flowing, contracting and expanding,
pain and joy, sun and moon,
beginning and ending.
The labour of love progressed.

And it was very good.

Our Father in Heaven

At the fifth time,
there was ceaseless activity:
fluttering
like the wings of the dove,
humming
like the murmuring of the dragonfly,
swimming
like the darting golden fish,
wriggling
like the lithe serpent,
surging
like the mighty lion.

And it was very good.

At the sixth time,
there was a momentary,
endless hesitation.
Then a child was born,
And the child looked just like the one
who had given it life.
The child, too,
was born with the power to create,
and to make decisions,
and to love.

The labourer looked
at all that had been accomplished,
and rejoiced,
for it was very good.

At the seventh time,
the labour was finished.

The task was complete,
and the labourer rested,
for she was very, very tired.

Kathy Galloway

18 Creation dance

In the beginning, God the dancer
danced the dance of love,
filling up the emptiness
of waiting with her rhythm.
She danced out the universe,
twirled the stars and planets,
held light and dark in either hand
and clasped them into wisdom.

And everything moved in a circle of love,
a circle of love, a circle of love.
And everything moved in a circle of love
and God saw that it was good.

Then God danced the mountains up
and trod the seas deep down.
She creased the land for rivers,
made rivers to hug the land.
Everywhere her footsteps went,
the earth broke into green,
flax and fern and tree and vine,
dancing to the rhythm of love.

And everything moved in a circle of love,
a circle of love, a circle of love.
And everything moved in a circle of love
and God saw that it was good.

When the earth was filled with the music
of every kind of creature,
God danced two people into being
and named them woman and man.
She sang to them, 'My children,
join me in creation.
Come and be my partners
dancing the dance of love.'

And everything moved in a circle of love,
a circle of love, a circle of love.
And everything moved in a circle of love
and God saw that it was good.

Joy Cowley
from *Psalms Down-Under* (Catholic Supplies [N.Z.])

19 *Bitter-Sweet*

Ah my dear angry Lord,
Since thou dost love, yet strike;
Cast down, yet help afford;
Sure I will do the like.
I will complain, yet praise;
I will bewail, approve:
And all my sour-sweet days
I will lament and love.

George Herbert

20 *Earth Prayer*

I am your mother: do not neglect me!
Children, protect me — I need your trust;
      my breath is your breath,
      my death is your death,
ashes to ashes, dust into dust.

I am your nurture: do not destroy me!
Love and enjoy me, savour my fruit;
      my good is your good,
      my food is your food,
water and flower, branches and root.

I am your lodging: do not abuse me!
Tenderly use me, soothing my scars;
      my health is your health,
      my wealth is your wealth,
shining with promise, set among stars.

God is our maker; do not deny God,
Challenge, defy God, threaten this place:
      life is to cherish —
      care or we perish!
I am your mother, tears on my face...

Shirley Erena Murray
Aotearoa, New Zealand

21 *Bio-centrism*

Western Christianity places human beings at the centre of the universe. The whole creation was created for the benefit of human beings, who are to dominate over the fish, the birds, and every living thing upon earth. Creation was condemned and cursed as a result of human sinfulness. But by the grace of God, human beings are offered the possibility of salvation. They, in turn, can save the planet by assuming responsibility as sons and daughters of God.

A contrasting way of understanding the world is by telling the story of the earth and the biosphere. As Thomas Berry has pointed out, the planet earth came into being about ten billion years ago, and life on the planet seven billion years later. Plants appeared about six hundred million years ago, and animals arrived a little later. Human consciousness only came some two million years ago. The biosphere existed long before us and its complexity has just begun to be understood by biologists in the twentieth century. It is arrogant on our part to think that the earth exists solely for our disposal, and that the salvation of this vast and expansive galaxy would depend on just five billion human beings.

Western anthropocentrism creates a God according to the image of human beings: God is king, father, judge and warrior. God is the Lord of history, intervening in human events. On the contrary, the Oriental and indigenous people who are tied to the soil imagine the divine, the Tao, as silent and non-intrusive. They speak of the earth with respect and reverence as the mother who is sustaining and life-affirming. A shift from anthropocentrism to bio-centrism necessitates a change in our way of thinking and speaking about God.

Kwok Pui-lan, Asia

22 Child-play

Father Mother God, *Dear*
every now and then you call me
to drop my burdens at the side of the road
and play games with you.
I respond sluggishly.
Carrying burdens can make me feel important
and sometimes I'm afraid to drop them
in case I suddenly become invisible.
But when I do let go for a while,
how simple life seems —
and how beautiful!

God of play and playfulness,
thank you for castles in the sand,
for swings and slides and soap bubbles,
kaleidoscopes, rainbows,
and wind to fly kites.
Thank you for child vision
of flowers and stones and water drops,
for child-listening to the universe
humming inside a seashell.
Thank you for showing me again,
a creation filled with laughter
and the enjoyment of your presence.
And thank you, thank you
dear Mother Father God
for the knowledge
of your enjoyment of me.

Joy Cowley
from Aotearoa Psalms (Catholic Supplies [N.Z.])

No Empty Phrases

Hallowed be your name

In the crowded street,
On the commuter train,
I saw His presence there

Moments of holiness

The Christ story

Versions of the Lord's Prayer

The Scottish traditional version

Our Father, which art in heaven,
hallowed be thy name;
thy kingdom come;
thy will be done in earth as it is in heaven.
Give us this day our daily bread,
*and forgive us our debts
as we forgive our debtors,
and lead us not into temptation
but deliver us from evil.
For thine is the kingdom, and the power, and the glory
for ever. Amen

some congregations say:

*   and forgive us our sins
    as we forgive those who sin against us.

23 *The Burning Bush*

I am a very small tree in a desert
and I am touched by the breath of God.
I don't ask for it. It just happens,
a suddenness inside me and then a presence
of wind and flame, burning, burning,
and I cover my eyes with my fears,
knowing that I am too small and too frail
to bear this firestorm of love.

I cry out, 'God, God, what are you doing?
I have always needed your Sunday warmth
but I can't cope with this searing
which feels like both heaven and hell.
You leave no part of me untouched.
That's not what I planned.
Please go away!'

There is no answer in the wind and flower,
but little by little, the blindness of my fear
is dissolved and I see with clear eyes
that the desert round me is no longer a desert.
It has been lit by the strong flame of love,
every bush, every tree transformed beyond itself.
I am not alone in this. I never was.
Every living thing has been summoned
to be on fire with the love of God
and to turn all barren places
into sacred ground.

Joy Cowley
from *Psalms Down-Under* (Catholic Supplies [N.Z.] Ltd.)

Moments

24 *At the Burning Bush*

But what if I
should hear that voice
practical,
earthy,
specific,
speaking to me?

What if God should say,
'I have heard,
I will save,
now you must hear
and go
and be the instrument
of my salvation.'

I want to stand
and see the glory of God,
to wonder,
worship
and be still...
but what if God says, 'Go!'?

Edmund Banyard

25 *Flower in the crannied wall*

Flower in the crannied wall,
I pluck you out of the crannies; —
Hold you here, root and all, in my hand,
Little flower — but if I could understand
What you are, root and all, and all in all,
I should know what God and man is.

Alfred, Lord Tennyson

26 *Not till my soul was dark*

I missed him when the sun began to bend;
I found him not when I had lost his rim;
With many tears I went in search of him,
Climbing high mountains which did still ascend,
And gave me echoes when I called my friend;
Through cities vast and charnel-houses grim,
And high cathedrals where the light was dim,
Through books and arts and works without an end,
But found him not — the friend whom I had lost.
And yet I found him — as I found the lark,
A sound in fields I heard but could not mark;
I found him nearest when I missed him most;
I found him in my heart, a life in frost,
A light I knew not till my soul was dark.

George Macdonald

27 *The silent gift*

We may not know the mystic's way
        on seas of fire
nor to far shores of union
        dare we aspire:
vainly we try to persevere
        yet rise no higher.

Just empty words we grasp as if
        stout rafts were there
for rescue — in a desperate bid
        to launch our prayer:
like drowning souls we struggle on —
        contact is rare.

Then strangely warm a rushing wind
        descends to bless
and fills with hope the sails that we
        had trimmed for less:
the gift comes to us silently —
        as we confess.

Margaret Connor

28 *Fleeting Presence*

In the crowded street,
On the commuter train,
I saw His Presence there.

In the news flash,
In the bleak rain,
Was God, beyond compare.

Caught up in commerce,
In the superstore,
I saw Him once again.

In the car crash,
With the homeless,
Was God, who shares our pain.

At my wits' end,
In the rush hour,
Was God, who keeps me sane,

Unexpected, uninvited,
Long ignored and long rejected,
He will come again.

David Adam

29 *Uniquely holy*

No Christian is holy as Christ is holy; freedom from sin is not yet complete in Christian experience. In themselves human beings are not worthy of life in full fellowship with God, nor capable of it. They need continual forgiveness and renewal as their means to freedom. They need power from God, sufficient to transform what they are, to sustain what they become, and to strengthen them for new deeds of faith and obedience. Through God's grace these needs are met, not once only but again and again in the lives of those actively committed to Christian discipleship. Christians therefore share that joy in living which the eternal God has in himself.

From A *Declaration of Faith*
The Congregational Church in England and Wales 1967

30 *'Lord, lord'*

'Lord', we say
not knowing who or what we're talking to
but willing to believe
something
bewildered
by everything
hoping
for anything
to validate our being
in a world that makes no sense
as we make no sense
unless it
and we
are yours.

when faith and hope flicker
like a candle flame
in the draughts of life,
when words deafen us,
through your silence
teach us love.

W. S. Beattie

31 *Immanuel*

Did Adam realise,
Lurking in the bushes full of shame,
What he had lost?
Did Eve remember,
Lying in the sweat of first-birth pain,
The seed of promise almost
Hidden by the sentence?
Maybe not.

Later, others who'd known nothing else,
Not heard him in the garden —
The cracking of small twigs underfoot,
The rustle of grass —
Others met him.
Unexpectedly he came
To Hagar in the desert
And Abraham under the huge trees.
All night Jacob struggled with the glorious stranger.
Moses was afraid at first;
Too bright a burning, too fierce
The heat of holiness.
Yet he became a friend,
Spoke face to face, began
To know as he was known.
Joshua the soldier met his captain;
Even Gideon was commissioned
And one day Manoah's wife
Surprised her husband.
Samuel listened; Daniel saw
At dead of night,
In the stillness,
Such a sight of future days
As threatened sanity

Meanwhile
In the womb of time
The promise grew. The seed
Took root in humble lime,
Davidic clay;
Began to sprout and bud
In men's minds, almost understood
By some to whom the word came.
They saw it
Growing as a righteous branch;
Unfurled before the nations
Like a banner, bringing distant islands
And scattered peoples
Home.

But they could not see
What lay between.
What lay in straw
And slept
Or cried with hunger.
Could not have foreseen
The unexpectedness of this.

Did Adam watch? And Eve?
And did they weep again,
This time with joy at such
Deliverance?
They had not thought
That he would live with them like this,
Inhabiting the world he made
So finally. Restoring all
Lost hope so permanently.
Coming, as always,
So unexpectedly.
Immanuel.

Judith Lyons

32 *Rich Beggars*

Lord, we are here
In the place we call your house
Trying to do this worship thing.

We are quite used to being here
Except sometimes we wonder
Whose idea it is
Yours, or our own?

Are we trying to buy your favour
By our loyalty and work?
Are we trying to win your approval
By making ourselves useful to you?

Let's be honest
At least, let's try.
We aren't that much use,
Not really,
Are we?

You don't say anything.
Neither the 'Yes' we want to hear
To make us feel good,
Nor the 'No'
That we are afraid of.

You do not answer.
Was it the right question?

Who are we to bargain with you?
Our hands are empty
As the hands of a new born baby,
Stretched out
Like the hands of someone dying.

Accept our worship, Lord
And us
On our knees before you
If so you please.

W. S. Beattie

33 *Presence*

Expecting Him, my door was open wide:
  Then I looked round
  If any lack of service might be found,
And saw Him at my side:
  How entered, by what secret stair,
  I know not, knowing only He was there.

T. E. Brown

34 *A Tenuous Joy*

I walk on air,
cloud-stepping heaven's shining span —
and yet with care
lest all my dreams should vanish in
despair.

When shall I know
the substance of these fragile hopes
which ebb and flow,
yet lure me on forever with
their glow?

Oh — hold me fast
in all my giddy skyward ways,
that first and last
Your touch will prove my vertigo
has passed!

Then calm and still
my joy shall be, not tenuous
but waiting, till
these wavering flights of mine fulfil
Your will.

Margaret Connor

35

Now I have known, O Lord,
What lies within my heart;
In secret, from the world apart,
My tongue hath talked with my Adored.

So in a manner we
United are, and One;
Yet otherwise disunion
Is our estate eternally.

Though from my gaze profound
Deep awe hath hid thy face
In wondrous and ecstatic grace
I feel thee touch my inmost ground.

Al Junaid of Baghdad 10th century

36 *The Good Spirit*

I was to be in this solitary cell for less than three months but after the first two or three weeks it felt as if I had slipped into a different time-scale. Days passed without any variation. The food-and-bathroom run and then nothing. I read and re-read everything available. I relived much of my life and made endless plans for the future. But after two months with not the slightest hint that I might be released I got more frightened. So many of my reflections had left me feeling inadequate that I began to doubt that I could cope alone.

One morning these fears became unbearable. I stood in the cell sinking into despair. I felt that I was literally sinking, being sucked down into a whirlpool. I was on my knees, gasping for air, drowning in hopelessness and helplessness. I thought that I was passing out. I could only think of one thing to say — 'Help me please, oh God, help me.' The next instant I was standing up, surrounded by a warm bright light. I was dancing, full of joy. In the space of a minute, despair had vanished, replaced by boundless optimism.

What had happened? I had never had any great faith, despite a Church of England upbringing. But I felt that I had to give thanks. But to what? Unsure of the nature of the experience, I felt most comfortable acknowledging the Good Spirit which seemed to have rescued me.

It gave me great strength to carry on and, more importantly, a huge renewal of hope — I was going to survive. Throughout my captivity, I would take comfort from this experience, drawing on it whenever optimism and determination flagged. In the euphoria of the next few days I felt completely confident. But soon I found myself wondering how, even with the support of a Good Spirit, I was going to manage alone.

John McCarthy

From *Some Other Rainbow* by John McCarthy and Jill Morrell

37 *An experience I shall always remember*

We had twelve men going to the Foreign Field in retreat with us last week, and a most wonderful Communion Service on Thursday night at ten thirty. It was half light and stormy and — as I broke the bread — I am informed that a sweep of birds sailed past the window as if trying to get in. I only know that when I was praying the intercession prayer with my eyes closed I heard steps coming towards the Table and opened my eyes in case someone was coming. There was no one there, but a wind rushed round me so real that I felt myself pressed backwards. It was a strange experience that I have communicated to no one here. Afterwards I remembered the old story that late at night monks will walk down the centre of the Church and can be seen walking right through the Communion Table. I saw nothing at all. But it is an experience I shall always remember whenever I administer the sacrament. It is the more remarkable as I was not feeling in the least eerie and certainly not anticipating any such experience. I like to take it as an omen that the thing is meant.

George MacLeod, founder of the Iona Community

38 *In Church*

The Church do seem a touching sight,
When folk a-coming in at door
Do softly tread the long-aisled floor
Below the pillared arches' height,
    With bells a-pealing,
    Folk a-kneeling,
Heart a-healing, wi' the love
An' peace a-sent 'em from above.

And there, wi' mild and thoughtful face,
Wi' down-cast eyes and voices dumb,
The old and young do slowly come
And take in stillness each his place;
    A-sinking slowly
    Kneeling lowly,
Seeking holy thoughts alone
In prayer before their Maker's throne.

William Barnes

39   *A Presence*

At times God had seemed so real and so intimately close. We talked not of a God in the Christian tradition but some force more primitive, more immediate and more vital, a presence rather than a set of beliefs. Our frankness underlined the reality of our feelings. We were both still trying to deal with the force and the weight of them. We prayed unashamedly, making no outward sign. We simply knew that each of us did pray and would on occasion remind each other to say a prayer for someone in particular among our families and lovers. In its own way our isolation had expanded the heart, not to reach out to a detached God but to find and become part of whatever 'God' might be. The energizing experience of another human being did not allow either of us to dwell too long on these matters, which were deep and unresolvable. We gave honestly of ourselves and of our experience and each received from the other with gratitude whatever was given. On occasion there would be discussions on vaguely religious themes, but they were certainly not confined by the dictates of strait-laced doctrines. We had each gone through an experience that gave us the foundations of an insight into what a humanized God might be.

Brian Keenan
From *An Evil Cradling*, the story of his imprisonment in Beirut

40   *At the centre of the market-place*

'I am not pleading political concern to the exclusion of the multifarious interests and obligations of men. I am not really arguing that the mother of five should leave them with a neighbour to address envelopes at Labour headquarters, or that the doctor should scamp his patients' lists to attend the Conservative convention, or that the artist should leave his studio to paint posters for the Economic League. I simply argue that the Cross be raised again at the centre of the market-place as well as on the steeple of the church. I am recovering the claim that Jesus was not crucified in a cathedral between two candles, but on a cross between two thieves; on the town garbage heap; at a crossroad so cosmopolitan that they had to write his title in Hebrew and in Latin and in Greek (or shall we say in English, in Bantu and in Afrikaans?); at the kind of place where cynics talk smut and thieves curse, and soldiers gamble. Because that is where churchmen should be and what churchmen should be about.'

George MacLeod, founder of the Iona Community

41 *Meeting for Worship*

Lord, when we try
to look and listen to you,
your light
beats on blind eyes —
our eyes.
Your word vibrates the air
around deaf ears —
our ears.

Not light, but yet a sort of warmth
on our upturned faces.
Not sound, yet something stirs
around us, through us, in us.

Something is being transmitted
not to be defined in words,
even such words as joy and hope and love;
a sense of being present
that reaches out between us
making our hearts real

W. S. Beattie

42 *Special Occasions*

Dutifully
we fill the pews,
hushed by the organ's lull,
then animatedly exchange our news
before the visiting preacher's entry:
'They say he comes from Hull.'

We sit on committees,
champion lost causes,
serve endless coffees,
collect for Christian Aid,
and in the pauses
hope to manage a sick call or two
before the supper's made.

We chase the dust
from nooks and crannies,
'do' the flowers, toll the bell,
welcome strangers,
transport the grannies,
then usually read a lesson or prayer
beside Brownies and Rangers
on special occasions.

Special Occasions?
Is it one today?
With this and that
then so much more,
we had forgotten
that flames
might leap up overhead,
and whirlwinds
lift us off the floor.

Margaret Connor

43 *A Wondrous Moment*

Dawn.
A rosebud sleeps, petal tightly furled;
Sepal fingers cupping it gently,
Protectingly,
Until,
Roused by the soft, warm flush of morning
A faint stirring signals its awakening.

Quietly I watch,
Fascinated, as, one by one
The sepals lose their hold;
Fall outward and down,
Folding over to form a pedestal
Upon which to display the ultimate glory
Of the rose — queen of the garden.

Slowly the bud expands,
With imperceptible speed pushing,
Pushing.
The vital urge to fulfil its destiny
Transcending all else.
See!
The tip is opening now.

Snap! — the minutest wisp of sound,
So clear and sharp I stare, amazed —
Joyously the first petal leaps away,
Revealing all the glowing loveliness
Of powdered carmine,
Velvet soft, delicately etched
Upon the purest gold.

Within this wondrous moment lies Eternity.

Nellie de Beaufort Saunders

Hallowed be your name

44 *A Moment in Eternity*

Like a fractured rainbow
Flashed a kingfisher's wing
In the suspension of a moment
I heard a skylark sing
A humming bee's soft organ notes
Accompanied the song
And the Aeolian harp
Of a gentle breeze
Stirred the trees to sing along
When a curlew joined
Its plaintive call
To the melody from the sky
The moment became adrift in time
As the memory of a sigh.

Charles Henry Stone

45 *Skylark*

Up, straight up he flew,
From the tufted ground,
A mile high,
Where held up only by atmosphere,
He exhaled his song,
An opera.
On every breath a note,
On every beat a breath,
Hung still like a hawk hunting,
A brown bit in mid air, a minstrel, a songster,
Unperturbed by the petrifying wind,
Flying only to be still there, to sing,
And ascending, was enveloped by the early morning,
The Heavenly billowy cloud.
Then only his song remained,
Feather and bone cast off with the earth,
But still, the trill,
A stellar song cast out of the cloud,
Poured from that celestial dome,
Pulled up my heart, with the skylark,
I followed with no thought of home.

Sasha Norris

46 *Of Seeing*

Oh! how little I have really seen
of what is around me.
Too much I have missed.
Too much I have over-looked.
In my haste to take in
all that I could,
I have not dwelt enough
And so have failed my memory's eye.
Failing to allow each detail
to etch itself into my brain
and denying myself the chance
to later re-create, with justice,
the object of that earlier pleasure
on the canvas of my mind.
To relive that visual moment.

Overawed by the sight
of a thousand roses,
I have not seen clearly the single rose,
the simple beauty of each petal.
Warmed and comforted by a blazing fire,
I have missed the colours in its flame.
In knowing, though poorly,
the colours and forms of landscape,
I have not noticed the fragile mosaics
created by the sky and the leaves of a birch
or the four petal perfection
and strength of pigment in a poppy.
Too casual has been my glance
and, therefore, too shallow my eye's acquaintance.
But now, with a blind man's hunger,
I must be more greedy of seeing.
Of seeing, not the whole panorama,
But the gentle detail of each optic sensation.

William Talbot

47

As for angels, I
know nothing of those with
      porcelain serenity
and wing-borne gravitas.
But I have heard
certain hints
rustlings and rumours; seen
the flickering of light
on shadowed corners; dignity
in suffering faces; felt
a sudden piercing stillness; smelt
in the dark night
scents of an
annunciation.

Kate Compston

The Christ Story

Annunciation

48 *Theotokos*

Unawares, I was drawn
into the soft, muted colours
that showed forth
the glorious message
that Gabriel announced
to the chosen God-bearer.
The graceful inclination of the head
spoke the humble accord
of her heart.
The flow of lines depicted
a life given to
receiving the fullness of divine love,
a life given to
letting go in order to give
birth to love in human form.

Puzzled, I cast about
in my mind as I tried to
decipher love's mysterious
language, whose Word conformed
not to the rules of human grammar
but to the wisdom of divine folly.
The manger was overshadowed
by the cross, at the foot of which
the soldier's sword pierced
the mother's heart
before she cradled her child
for the first and last time.

Fearful, I hesitated
before the Word
that was revealed
unto me.
And then
I bowed my head
and inclined my heart
as Mary did.

Julia Bebbington

49 *Mary: proto-disciple and woman*

Mary has been depicted as silent, sweet, self-effacing, docile, passive, submissive, A Mater Dolorosa. Actually, this portrayal of Mary is a masculine perception of idealized femininity which has been inflicted on us and which many of us in turn have tried hard to internalize. In recent times, however, women have begun to appropriate the Bible for themselves without the mediation of male interpreters, and realize how Mary has been misrepresented. They see Mary of the Gospels, especially of the Magnificat, as a woman of faith and intelligence, who is gentle and attentive, yet decisive and responsive, a woman of deep compassion but also of great courage, who is able to take initiatives and make great sacrifices, and is willing to risk in order to accomplish God's word and will. This is to a growing number of women, and should be to us, the true Mary, who is proto-disciple, yes, but above all, woman.

Virginia Fabella
From *New Eyes for Reading*

50 *To Mary, my mother*

All-knowing mother, gentle flesh,
flesh of my flesh, source of my life;
    I lie in weakness in your bosom strength
    as you enfold my infant years.

Unknowing mother, blind still to future years,
where will you be, what will you feel
    the day that nails press deep my flesh
    and life ebbs out in gasping pain and weakening loss?
Will your flesh feel the sharpness of the thorns;
your spirit know the thrust of bloodied spear?
And shall we find new kinship in our pain?

'Mother of God'; the creeds will name your name.
And truly so.
Yet am I not your mother, too;
your mother, father, friend and Lord
as in my death-denying years, matured by pain
I fast become what I already am:
the true fulfilment of all human love;
which is itself divine?

Donald Hilton

51 *Virgin Birth*

We have within us a virgin place,
A holy space which belongs to God alone.
We know it by its hunger,
We name it by its need,
The space which will not be touched
By the people we love
Or the things we gather
Or the positions we hold.

We have within us a growing place,
An eternal space that exists for Truth,
Where the love of God overcomes us,
Where the life of God fills us,
The Emmanuel space where we conceive
And become pregnant of the Holy One
And day by day, give birth
To Christ in the world.

Joy Cowley
from *Psalms Down-Under* (Catholic Supplies [N.Z.] Ltd.)

52 *Nativity*

He it turns out is free as we are not,
a bell without a flaw, a note so pure
we could not pitch it. She after all
was not married when the spiteless
offspring of other unions migrated.
It never occurred before, no human ear
could witness such a birth, no elephant
from its side delivered one so ordinary.
Only camels knew him and lambs
and butterflies, for God escapes all
but the lost eye, the ladened back,
ragged fleece and ephemeral wings.

Ron Parker

53 *A shepherd's tale*

I hesitate to speak
    lest some will mock
the telling of my tale
    or try to rock
the steady quest of my
    long life's intent
by focussing on many
    an argument.
They miss my vision's light
    and try to stall
by saying, 'That is not
    the way at all.'

Yet I will always hold
    those shining hours
on distant hills with dawn
    about to flower
and all my flocks full fed
    upon new ground.
Then former hopes returned
    to circle round
so that I caught each one
    on dazzling wing
and in my wonder heard
    the angels sing.

Margaret Connor

54 *This poverty*

I think in this the Magi were most wise,
That, when they knelt before humility,
They realised it was no disguise
But revelation of divinity.
Only the very greatest love of all
Could seek its showing in a babe so small —
This poverty was God's Epiphany.

Father Andrew

55 *Christmastide*

In the moontime of the winter,
when the sun redly rises;
in the moontime of the winter,
when the trees starkly stretch,
then, O Christ, you come:
softly as a gently falling snowflake,
with the lusty energy of a newborn boy,
the blood and pain of your coming,
staining the distant horizon.

In the frost of the starlight,
when the sun gives way to the moon,
in the frost of the starlight,
when the earth is turned to stone,
then, O Christ, you come:
slowly as the rhythm of the seasons,
quickly as the rushing of cradling waters,
worshipped by the wise,
adored by the humble,
the ecstatic joy of your coming,
heralding songs of peace.

Into the world of the refugee and the soldier,
the soles of your feet have touched the ground.
Into the world of the banker and beggar,
the soles of your feet have touched the ground.
Into the world of Jew and Arab,
the soles of your feet have touched the ground.

Walk with us, saviour of the poor,
be a light on our way,
travel beside the weary,
fill the broken hearted with hope
and heal the nations,
that all may walk
in the light of the glory of God.

Kate McIlhagga

56 *St. Patrick's Hymn*

Christ, as a light,
Illumine and guide me!
Christ, as a shield, o'ershadow and cover me!
Christ be under me! Christ be over me!
Christ be beside me
On left hand and right!
Christ be before me, behind me, about me!
Christ this day be within and without me!

Christ, the lowly and meek,
Christ, the All-powerful, be
In the heart of each to whom I speak,
In the mouth of each who speaks to me!
In all who draw near me,
Or see me or hear me!

At Tara to-day, in this awful hour,
I call on the Holy Trinity!
Glory to Him who reigneth in power,
The God of the elements, Father, and Son,
And Paraclete Spirit, which Three are the One,
The ever-existing Divinity!

Salvation dwells with the Lord,
With Christ, the Omnipotent Word.
From generation to generation
Grant us, O Lord, Thy grace and salvation!

James Clarence Mangan

57 *The Anonymous Christ*

I sat all day,
in the shade of the banyan tree,
turning my face
to the distant hills, and waited
for my Lord to come
My heart pounded heavily
with expectation
and my eyes burned.
The morning passed away
and the noon melted
into evening and the evening
into darkness.
But he did not come.

I recalled that a poor mother
and her child passed by that way,
then an old man with a bundle of
firewood and later
a traveller who lost his way.
I hardly even looked at them.
At the fall of night
I went into my hut
and lay awake on my bed
with a heavy heart
and then I heard a voice
saying
'I passed by you thrice
but you did not see me.'

Solomon Raj, India

58 *Completely like us*

If Christ had become incarnate now
    and were a thirty-year-old man today,
he could be here in this cathedral
    and we wouldn't know him from the rest of you —
a thirty-year-old man, a peasant from Nazareth,
    here in the cathedral like any peasant
    from our countryside.
The Son of God made flesh would be here
    and we wouldn't know him —
        one completely like us.

Oscar Romero

59 One Friday in Eternity

Death

One Friday in Eternity
A man was framed they say,
A man was framed, but why the fuss,
It happens every day;
With all the trappings of the law
It happens every day;
One Friday in Eternity
Repeated every day.

One Friday in Eternity
A man was flogged they say,
A man was flogged, but why the fuss,
It happens every day;
Imprisoned, brainwashed,
    tortured, starved,
It happens every day.
One Friday in Eternity
Repeated every day.

One Friday in Eternity
A man was hung they say,
A man was hung, but why the fuss,
It happens every day;
Hung, shot or crucified, who cares,
It happens every day.
One Friday in Eternity
Repeated every day.

One Friday in Eternity
That man was God they say,
If that is true — if God was there —
It happens every day;
If God is sharing mortal pain
It happens every day.
One Friday in Eternity
Repeated every day.

Edmund Banyard

60 Holy Friday

The conflict of Light with Darkness is finished. For a moment Darkness seemed to prevail: 'This is your hour and the power of darkness' (Luke 22.15). But the fight was fought out and the victory won: 'It is finished' (19.30).

The date of the triumph of love is Good Friday, not Easter Day. Yet if the story had ended there, the victory would have been barren. What remains is not to win it, but to gather in its fruits. Consequently St. John does not present the Resurrection as a mighty act by which the hosts of evil are routed, but rather as the quiet rising of the sun which has already vanquished night. The atmosphere of the story has all the sweet freshness of dawn on a spring day.

William Temple

61 *Bear well the hurt*

Suffering Lord,
Now you know it all:
    the pain that grips the body in untimely death,
    the agony of bloody wounds,
    the tortured limbs,
    and that deep sense of frail humanity.

Forsaken Lord,
You know it all:
    rejection at the hands of men,
    the fleeing footsteps of once-close friends,
    the clink of thirty pieces in the purse,
    the callous glance of soldiers' eyes, committed to cold duty,
    neglect and scorn, pressed hard within the hour of need,
    and a devastating loss of God.

Lonely Lord,
You know it all:
    the scapegoat's banishment,
    the visionary's isolation,
    the curt dismissal of an alien world,
    and the pain-filled misunderstanding of those called friends.

Suffering, forsaken, lonely Lord,
bear well the hurt, the pain, the loss
for us, and for all human seed.
The world must have just one
obedient to the end;
the Chosen One.

Thanks be to God.

Donald Hilton

62 *Easterings*

Every hour of every day there are crucifixions,
the Christ on trial in someone, somewhere,
judged in fear, condemned in ignorance,
mocked and beaten, imprisoned, killed,
while we watch at the foot of the cross
or from three cock crows away, and ask,
'God, God, why have you forsaken them?'

The world is full of Good Fridays and Golgothas.
In the small arena of our lives,
there appears to be the same defeat of goodness
and it's difficult to wear a bright smile
when the heart hangs heavy in a darkness
full of thorns and nails and swords.
Unable to see beyond dyings, we cry,
'God, God, why have you forsaken us?'

Then something happens. Easter Sunday happens.
This movement within, this turning, breaking,
this earthquake shift through an old fault line.
A cosmic birth happens, darkness to light,
God dancing on pierced feet to make a celebration
of all our dyings, even our little ones,
so that we can see, this side of the tomb,
that there are no endings, only transformations,
as we grow towards the source of our being.

In that moment of knowing, we see all of life
wrapped up in the wholeness of Easter,
and in awe we silently pray,
'God, God, you have never forsaken us.'

Joy Cowley
from *Psalms Down-Under* (Catholic Supplies [N.Z.] Ltd.)

63 *Easter Sonnet*

Rising

Dawn breaks in the garden. Flowers unfold
Their petals to the sun. Birds shake their wings
And preen for day. Nocturnal cold
Slowly gives way to warmth. Living things
Drowsily stretch and yawn. A lizard's tongue
Darts at a fly. A busy buzzing bee
Bumbles from bush to bush. Beetles among
The gravel rustle and scurry. Rasping, a key
Turns in the gate. The garden, now awake
Growing and hunting, pauses, holds its breath
Suspended as the mourning women take
Their path towards the tomb to honour death
Stumble, and cry in fear at first sight
Of the cave's mouth, alive with dazzling light.

Brigid Somerset

64 *Freedom*

The dark doubts of the winter months are past
And Easter, young and green, is here at last.
The April morning grass is bless'd with dew
And palest sun shines out of palest blue.
The old sheep stroll, the young lambs leap and play —
    O, blessed is the lamb newborn today.
The withered root entombed beneath the earth
Puts out new shoots and joins the great rebirth.
The Spring is here, the egg, the grain, the seed:
And from them the imprisoned life is freed;
From Winter's cold grave, Spring's new life appears
And echoes his resurrection through the years.

Katherine Middleton

Hallowed be your name

65 Easter Sunday

This is the day of festival
and we thank you, O God of celebration,
with hymns of praise rising like balloons
and banners of love waving from our hearts.
Today we dance with the angels
round all the empty tombs in our lives,
celebrating transformation,
from grief to laughter,
from darkness into light.
Today we glimpse the truth
of suffering and death
as we move with you in your Jesus song
of resurrections without end.

Joy Cowley
from *Psalms Down-Under* **(Catholic Supplies [N.Z.] Ltd.)**

66 Dead and Alive

Dead, Lord, they said, dead and buried;
and the new truth of your presence leapt into their lives.
Gone, they said, gone. Gone for ever;
and there you were, present in heart and community.
Finished, they said, finished. Finished and forgotten;
and your friends found you in a garden, in a room, on a road.
Lost, they said, lost. Lost and gone for ever;
and your Church today proclaims your eternal presence and abiding love.

Alive, we say, alive and living.
Here, we say, here and always.
Fulfilled, we say, fulfilled and completed.
The heartbeat of the world throbs again;
Christ reborn from the grave
and we his friends with him.

Donald Hilton

67 *Because Christ rose...*

Ethel Mulvaney was a Canadian working with the Red Cross in Singapore when it fell to the Japanese on February 15th 1942. She was interned in Changi Jail. As the first Easter approached she petitioned the Prison Commandant for permission for a group of women to sing in the courtyard (so that all could hear) on Easter morning.

'Why?' demanded the officer.

'Because Christ rose from the dead on Easter morning!' she replied.

'Request denied', he barked, 'return to your compound.'

This drama of request and refusal was made twelve times as Easter drew nearer. Each time, Ethel Mulvaney suffered the same rough manhandling. Then, to their utter astonishment and joy, the day before the Sunday, came the order over the loud-speakers: 'Women prisoners may sing for five minutes in courtyard No. 1 at dawn tomorrow.' For five precious minutes the women praised God in song for the raising-up of Jesus. In that hell they sang of their hope and of what was a fact in their experience. Silently, they filed back to their compound.

As they passed through a gateway a guard stepped up to Ethel, and from inside his brown tunic he drew out a tiny orchid. Handing it to her he whispered in broken English: 'He is risen indeed!'

Anon

68 *Encounter*

We picked him up just out of Slough —
he looked honest enough
and anyhow we needed the company.
Sometimes it's easier
to confide in a stranger
and it helped
that he seemed to know nothing
of recent events in the City.

Two coffees on at the first Services,
we began to unravel
the disillusionment of our days,
and laid on him
the agony of our abandoned hopes.
But he forced us to think again —
and we didn't want to think —
we'd had enough of ecstasy and pain.

We should have left him there —
this stranger who offered no peace —
yet something impelled us
to carry him on,
and then, considering the hour,
we invited him to share a meal
at Milton Keynes.

Later, as we relived the wonder
of discovering his identity,
we shuddered too, knowing
how easily
we might have missed him.

Margaret Connor

69   *Wind and Fire*

Pentecost

The fire of the Spirit was not a general flame,
not bushfire, contagious, engulfing all.
But a flame on each one.
So we never carry the flame
from place to place,
as though the Spirit is our private box of matches
or our little incense pot.

But the fire is there, already, now.
It shines in the eyes of the eager,
joyful trusting children of God.
It is there in the hands of the healers
and servers and bearers of heavy loads.
It is local. A flame on each one.

There is also the wind, and the wind travels;
across oceans and mountains, always in movement.
May God let us be the breezes of the Spirit,
which fan the flames and fill the house
and let the smoking flax burst into a glory of fire.

> Wind and fire, life of the Spirit,
> universal and local, be our energy;
> wind and fire, elements of Pentecost,
> power for the Kingdom, be power for our city.

Bernard Thorogood

70 *Wild Goose*

I am always restless —
Onwards, upwards, ever travelling,
Never stopping for long;
Active and urgent in my mission.

Coming to rest
On enquirers:
Men and women,
Many and varied, differing needs,
Uplifting their spirits,
Nourishing deep hopes,
In-planting the seed of truth,
Transforming the timid and weak.
Yes! I am the Wild Goose; Spirit of God.

Y Mochyn Daear

71 *I AM*

I am the wind which breathes upon the sea,
I am the wave of the ocean,
I am the murmur of the billows,
I am the ox of the seven combats,
I am the vulture on the rocks,
I am the beam of the sun,
I am the fairest of the plants,
I am a wild boar in valour,
I am a salmon in the water,
I am a lake in the plain,
I am a word of science,
I am the point of the lance in battle,
I am the God who creates in the head the fire.
Who is it that throws light into the meeting on the mountain?
Who announces the ages of the moon?
Who teaches the place where couches the sun?

Anon

72 *A Present Fire*

Not for us the singed heads
　　with upturned faces
seen in arenas where apostles
　　congregated —
in more familiar places
　　we have awaited
our baptism of fire.

In neat suburban semis
　　by rolling fairways,
in inner city flats
　　up concrete stairways,
in banks and stores,
　　on foundry floors,
in launderettes
　　and Special Schools,
on broad lawned campuses
　　and in the typing pools —

we have heard the singing
　　of high hopes.

Not only in a hurricane
　　of tongues comes
our illusive revelation,
　　heaven riven:
for the most part quietly,
　　yet valid still,
the present fire is given.

Margaret Connor

73   *Always Pentecost*

It will always be Pentecost in the church,
provided the church lets the beauty of the Holy Spirit
shine forth from her countenance.
When the church ceases to let her strength rest
on the power from above that Christ promised her
and that he gave her on that day,
and when the church leans rather on the weak forces
of the power or the wealth of this earth,
then the church ceases to be newsworthy.

The church will be fair to see,
perennially young,
attractive in every age,
as long as she is faithful
to the Spirit
through her communities
through her pastors,
through her very life.

Oscar Romero

No Empty Phrases

Your kingdom come

Your kingdom come ... Your will be done

The expression of similar ideas in consecutive phrases may be an example of the Jewish literary form with which we are familiar from the Book of Psalms e.g.

He does not deal with us according to our sins.
nor repay us according to our iniquities.
Psalm 103. 10

The intention of this form is to reinforce the affirmation by repetition but in a way that enriches and enlarges the sentiment rather than simply repeating it. Matthew, but not Luke, uses this double-action form and if, as is often supposed, Matthew wrote his Gospel primarily with a Jewish readership in mind, it would be natural for him to use a Jewish style of writing. Luke, writing more for a Gentile readership, would not feel the same compulsion.

In selecting material for these two sections in this anthology a distinction has been loosely — and probably arbitrarily — drawn between first, the initiative and action (or seeming inaction) of God towards creating a kingdom for the fulfilment of which we can only pray: Your kingdom come!

In the second section (Your will be done...) the material reflects our human contribution, as by discipleship, action, prayer, and thoughtfulness we seek to work for the fulfilment of the purposes of God.

Seeds of the kingdom

As if God was not there

The nature of the kingdom

Versions of the Lord's Prayer

The Authorized Bible versions (1611)

Our Father which art in heaven,
Hallowed be thy name.
Thy kingdom come.
Thy will be done in earth as it is in heaven.
Give us this day our daily bread.
And forgive us our debts,
as we forgive our debtors.
And lead us not into temptation,
but deliver us from evil:
For thine is the kingdom, and the power, and the glory,
for ever. Amen

Matthew 6. 9b – 13

Our Father which art in heaven,
Hallowed be thy name.
Thy kingdom come.
Thy will be done,
as in heaven so in earth.
Give us day by day our daily bread.
And forgive us our sins;
for we also forgive everyone that is indebted to us.
And lead us not into temptation;
but deliver us from evil.

Luke 11. 2b – 4

74 *Thy Kingdom Come*

Seeds of the kingdom

In the quiet of the morning,
In the new day that is dawning,
Thy Kingdom come.

In my waking and my dressing,
In my life and its progressing,
Thy Kingdom come.

In this moment for the taking,
In the things that I am making,
Thy Kingdom come.

In the people I am meeting,
In each one I shall be greeting,
Thy Kingdom come.

In my tasks and my employment,
In my leisure and enjoyment,
Thy Kingdom come.

All day, until its very ending,
Praise to you I shall be sending,
Thy Kingdom come.

David Adam

Your kingdom come

75 Sometimes

Sometimes things don't go, after all,
from bad to worse. Some years, muscadel
faces down frost; green thrives; the crops don't fail,
sometimes a man aims high, and all goes well.

A people sometimes will step back from war;
elect an honest man; decide they care
enough, that they can't leave some stranger poor.
Some men become what they were born for.

Sometimes our best efforts do not go
amiss; sometimes we do as we meant to.
The sun will sometimes melt a field of sorrow
that seemed hard frozen; may it happen for you.

Sheenagh Pugh

76 Once in a life-time

History says, *Don't hope*
On this side of the grave.
But then, once in a lifetime
The longed for tidal wave
Of justice can rise up,
And hope and history rhyme.

So hope for a great sea-change
On the far side of revenge.
Believe that a further shore
Is reachable from here.
Believe in miracles
And cures and healing wells.

From *Philoctetes* by Sophocles
translated by Seamus Heaney

77 *Celebrate the promise*

In the midst of hunger and war
    we celebrate the promise of plenty and peace.
In the midst of oppression and tyranny
    we celebrate the promise of service and freedom.
In the midst of doubt and despair
    we celebrate the promise of faith and hope.
In the midst of fear and betrayal
    we celebrate the promise of joy and loyalty.
In the midst of hatred and death
    we celebrate the promise of love and life.
In the midst of sin and decay
    we celebrate the promise of salvation and renewal.
In the midst of death on every side
    we celebrate the promise of the living Christ.

World Council of Churches 1983 Assembly Worship Book

78 *Because*

Some things don't just happen
like Christmas comes;
some things only happen
like beautiful flowers
as the sun and rain say yes
and they happen because.

Cecily Taylor

79 *Peace Process*

From a compost heap
rises a tender shoot —
waste slowly turning
to fertile ground.

In a stark landscape
peace lifts a fragile shoot;
may all rains be gentle
no winds blow.

Cecily Taylor

80 *A Seed on the Wind*

My father told me about God.
He said, The city where we live
is a city without peace.
But there will come a city
filled with peace
and it will cover the whole world...

There shall be no more rich and poor,
no kings, no slaves,
no more hunger, no more aggression,
but light enough and bread for everyone.
That is God's dream, what God wills.

I shivered from happiness,
and each time I heard these words
it was the same.
My father said,
that city people build by doing good.
God is the still small voice within
that speaks to you
and tells you what is good
in a voice that you can understand,
so that you know how to do right
for the one who is beside you.

Not because blind fate
rules this universe,
not because the world is poor
and nature vicious,
but because the strongest rule,
and the strong kill the weak,
and those with money and power
desire still more —
that is why the world topples.

You who live in this godforgotten world,
do not forget who you are yourself:
a drop of water, a seed on the wind,
flowers in the open field,
sharer of all.

But also remember his name — 'God of the poor' —
and remember the son of man
who was the spokesman for that God,
and seek a place where people
speak and live in his spirit.
And learn to understand that voice
that speaks to you from far off and within
to tell you what is good.
So that you choose to stand on the side of the poor,
and to walk down their road.

Huub Oosterhuis

81 *Before Life and After*

A time there was — as one may guess
And as, indeed, earth's testimonies tell —
Before the birth of consciousness,
When all went well.

None suffered sickness, love, or loss,
None knew regret, starved hope, or heart-burnings;
None cared whatever crash or cross
Brought rack to things.

If something ceased, no tongue bewailed,
If something winced and waned, no heart was wrung;
If brightness dimmed, and dark prevailed,
No sense was stung.

But the disease of feeling germed,
And primal rightness took the tinct of wrong;
Ere nescience shall be reaffirmed
How long, how long?

Thomas Hardy

Your kingdom come

82 *A time that was*

When I was young
my world appeared a simpler place
than now.
George Dixon was the pianist
whose music gave discreet accompaniment
to boys and girls come out to play,
and fork-ploughed farmer's fields
on shepherd's pie;
when Mother baked, and ironed,
and listened.

This was a time when questions could be asked
and answers given,
when freedom was the natural, easy friend
of place and order;
when love without self-consciousness
occurred as readily as heat bumps
on pale freckled summer skin.

Was age the subvert of this world —
the tidal wash of adolesce
dissolving careful castles built of sand?
Or did the family's growing wealth allow
transition from the stony level hard times
to the prosperous slopes upon the mountain of excess?

This world of middle wealth and middle age
is set amidst the language of exchange
to tunes too harsh and broken for George Dixon's fluid touch.
Though I wonder if the goods and pace which seep into
the void once filled by place and love
can ever satisfy or compensate for what is lost?

Perhaps, perhaps it is the child-grown-man,
yet child at heart,
who must recover for the sake of those now aged,
and re-present as gift,
the memory and so the presence of the time that was.

Ian Fosten

83 *The Lesson (an anti-pastoral)*

The small schoolgirl
   on her way down
      grey Portugal Lane
         late for class
who brushes a careless
   hand against
     the one green
         nettle that had to sprout
    from yards of concrete
can't believe
   there's no dock leaf
       to cancel
       it out.

Tracy Ryan

*As if God was
not there*

84 *Sonnet: On his blindness*

When I consider how my light is spent,
   Ere half my days, in this dark world and wide,
   And that one talent which is death to hide,
Lodged with me useless, though my soul more bent
To serve therewith my maker, and present
   My true account, lest he returning chide,
   Doth God exact day-labour, light denied?
   I fondly ask; but Patience to prevent
That murmur, soon replies, God doth not need
Either man's work or his own gifts, who best
   Bear his mild yoke, they serve him best, his state
Is kingly. Thousands at his bidding speed
   And post o'er land and ocean without rest:
   They also serve who only stand and wait.

John Milton

85 *As if you were not there*

As if you were not there,
The skies ignite and thunder,
Rivers tear their banks asunder,
Thieves and nature storm and plunder:
All beware,
As if you were not there.

As if you were not there,
Famine and flood together
Usher death, disease and terror;
Stricken mothers wonder whether
God heeds prayer,
As if you were not there.

As if you were not there,
We televise the dying,
Watch the helpless victims crying,
Salve our consciences by sighing,
'Life's unfair!'
As if you were not there.

As if you were not there,
Your Son, when faith defied him,
Faced a crowd which crucified him,
Leaving friends who had denied him
In despair,
As if you were not there.

Because he rose again
And showed God's love is vaster
Than the ultimate disaster,
We entreat you now to master
Strife and pain,
Because he rose again.

John L Bell and Graham Maule

86 *God's inaction*

I did not return home after the verdict. Although others were in a festive mood and eager to celebrate, I knew the authorities could strike at any moment, and I did not want to give them the opportunity. I was anxious to be off before I was banned or arrested, and I spent a night in a safe house in Johannesburg. It was a restless night in a strange bed, and I started at the sound of every car, thinking it might be the police...

...That night I addressed a meeting of African township ministers in Cape Town. I mention this because the opening prayer of one of the ministers has stayed with me over these many years and was a source of strength at a difficult time. He thanked the Lord for His bounty and goodness, for His mercy and His concern for all men. But then he took the liberty of reminding the Lord that some of his subjects were more downtrodden than others, and that it sometimes seemed as though He was not paying attention. Then the minister said that if the Lord did not show a little more initiative in leading the black man to salvation, the black man would have to take matters into his own hands. Amen.

Nelson Mandela, from *Long Walk to Freedom*

87 *God's neglect*

Look down from heaven and see, from your holy and glorious habitation.
Where are your zeal and might?
The yearning of your heart and your compassion?
They are withheld from me.
For you are our father, though Abraham does not know us,
and Israel does not acknowledge us
you, O Lord, are our father; our redeemer from of old is your name.
Why, O Lord, do you make us stray from your ways and harden our heart,
so that we do not fear you?
Turn back for the sake of your servants
for the sake of the tribes that are your heritage.
Your holy people took possession for a little while;
but now our adversaries have trampled down your sanctuary.
We have long been like those whom you do not rule,
like those not called by your name.
O that you would tear open the heavens and come down,
so that the mountains would quake at your presence —
as when fire kindles brushwood and the fire causes water to boil —
to make your name known to your adversaries,
so that the nations might tremble at your presence.

Isaiah 63. 15 – 64. 2 (NRSV)

88 *No special treatment*

When God pulls down what he built up,
and roots up what he planted,
then friends of his must take their luck:
no special treatment's granted.

When God sends ruin on the land,
the outcome there's no saying;
you must take your life in hand
and search for strength in praying.

Jeremiah 45. 4–5
translated by H.J.Richards

89 *Out of This*

Out of this confusion,
this interminable tangle
of uncertain days,
I call you.

Out of nights ghosted
by insidious whispers
of past transgressions,
I call you.

Out of this chaos,
my token resolutions
broken again and again,
I call you.

But when I see
black buds break through
on battered branches,
I hear you.

As aconites rise
brave above last drifts
of greying snow,
I hear you.

And slowly
I begin to know
a personal resurrection.

Margaret Connor

90 *God in failure*

Let us not pray to be sheltered from dangers,
but to be fearless in facing them.
Let us not beg for the stilling of pain,
but for the heart to conquer it.
Let us not look for allies in life's battlefield,
but to our own strength.
Let us not crave in anxious fear to be saved,
but hope for the patience to win freedom.
Grant that we may not be cowards, O Lord,
feeling your mercy in our success alone;
but let us find the grasp of your hand
in our failures.

Rabindranath Tagore, India

91 *Suffering*

If I had not suffered
I would not have known
   the love of God.

If many people had not suffered
God's love would not have been
   passed on.

If Jesus had not suffered
God's love would not have been
   made visible.

Mizuno Genzo, Japan

92

O Christ, the Master Carpenter,
who at the last through wood and nails
purchased our whole salvation;
wield well your tools in the workshop of your world,
so that we, who come rough-hewn to your bench,
may here be fashioned to a truer beauty by your hand.

Source unknown

93 *Kingdom Come*

No king shall rule but he who serves,
No servant lack what he deserves,
For in God's realm of kingdom-come
The king and servant shall be one.

His kingly rule means equal law,
In every land hope for the poor,
A freedom to express the mind,
To follow conscience unconfined.

His kingly rule concludes old wars,
Using all gifts to speed his cause;
His rule is seen as ceaseless care
For all God's people everywhere.

His servanthood is known as peace;
The heart, obedient, finds release.
He meets the thirsty with a cup;
The fallen, found, he raises up.

His servanthood is sharing pain;
The suffering know this brother's name.
He carries loads, he takes our sin
As God's own grief, as wounds for him.

Our servant-king reigns from the cross,
Declaring life is won through loss;
Life for the world is dearly won
By him who makes the kingdom come.

Bernard Thorogood

The nature of the kingdom

94 *(Reluctant Leadership)*

Please don't call me Expert
and I'll speak of what I've learned,
I'll show you what I've seen
and open, if I dare, for you my thoughts.

Please don't call me Boss,
for I can offer no authority
without the test of your experience
and honest facing of the questions posed.

Please offer me no deference
but save it for the bell-sound
which rings true when others' lived-through insight
chimes harmoniously with yours.

Be sparing of your trust of me,
conserve it for that richer seam
of truth, of purpose, and of love
of which my life may have displayed a fitful gleam.

If I am here for you, and others too,
it is as fellow-traveller (and one whose feet are often sore)
for whom the call to journey and the view of promised lands
came sooner, surer, clearer than for you;
that's all.

Ian Fosten

95 *The Leader*

I wanna be the leader
I wanna be the leader
Can I be the leader?
Can I? I can?
Promise? Promise?
Yippee, I'm the leader
I'm the leader

OK what shall we do?

Roger McGough

Your kingdom come

96 *Bowl and towel*

We confess it, Lord;
King of the castle we would love to be:
with servants at our beck and call;
our word the law,
our wishes granted,
and every whim and fancy met.

We confess it, Lord;
First in the contest we would love to be:
chosen before others,
winning every game,
applauded, cheered, acclaimed.

We confess it, Lord;
Front of the queue we would love to be:
first pick of the food,
vintage of the wine,
best seats at the table.

> And then you come.
> You kneel before our pride; you wash our feet.
> You offer bread and wine, equally to all,
> and call us friends, with no distinction made.

The castle walls are breached by love,
The team renewed in glad co-operation.
The table's round, the seats are free.
And welcomed by forgiving love,
we eat and drink with grateful hearts.

Donald Hilton

97   *The Beatitudes*

How lucky you are if you are poor!
God will make you rich!

How lucky you are if you're not very important!
God will make you great!

How lucky you are if your heart has been broken!
It will mend even stronger!

How lucky you are if you're starving!
You'll get all you want, and more!

How lucky you are if you're tender with others!
You know how tender God really is!

How lucky you are if you're straight with people!
You see God very clearly indeed!

How lucky you are if you make friends with people!
You've brought a bit of heaven to earth!

How lucky you are if people hate you
   for standing up for what is right!
A new world can be built on people like you!

H. J. Richards

98   *God's sovereignty*

It is with wisdom, love, power and serenity that God knows and cares and rules throughout his universal domain. We speak about each attribute in turn, but each time with the rest in view. For it is in the expression of his love, made effective by his power and arising from his serenity, that God is seen to be wise. It is because he is wise and powerful and serene in his loving that we can entrust ourselves to him with a love responding to his own. We look to his power with confidence and hope because the power of God is the practice of wisdom and love grounded in serenity. We acknowledge his serenity with thanksgiving, for if his wisdom, love and power were not conceived in peace and joy they would not bring to the realm of God the full joy and peace which he promises.

from *A Declaration of Faith*
The Congregational Church in England and Wales 1967

99 *The Devil's Beatitudes*

Blessed are those who are too tired, busy or disorganised
    to meet with other Christians on Sunday each week —
        they are my best workers.

Blessed are those who enjoy noticing the mannerisms of clergy, choir and
servers —
        I can see their heart is not in it.

Blessed are the Christians who wait to be asked
    and expect to be thanked —
        I can use them.

Blessed are the touchy —
    with a bit of luck they can even stop going to church.

Blessed are those who keep themselves
    and their time and their money
    to themselves —
        they are my missionaries.

Blessed are those who claim to love their God
    at the same time as hating other people —
        they are mine for ever.

Blessed are the troublemakers —
    they shall be called my children.

Blessed are those who have no time to pray —
    they are easy prey to me.

Blessed are you when you read this
    and think it is about other people and not about yourself —
I've got you!

Anon

100 *God's Great Highway*

Let desert wastes rejoice and bloom,
Their sands sing out with joy
For God's great highway shall pass through,
And death shall be destroyed.
Instead, the streams of life shall flow
Through green and fertile fields,
The seeds of love his hand shall sow,
Their fruits his power reveal.

In lives discouraged and unfilled
Hope shall at last be found;
Upon the top of Calvary hill
The prisoners are unbound,
And as the powers stood to cheer,
The dumb began to cry,
The blind could see, the deaf could hear
The cripples dancing by.

The Road of Holiness is here
For those who would be saved
And those who used to shake with fear
Can stand now with the brave;
Together travel on that road
And make the deserts sing
A song of joy, a song to God,
The ever-loving King.

Colin Ferguson

101 The Barony, Glasgow

The national Church of Scotland, which had once commanded the allegiance of the bulk of the people of Scotland, was by 1843 reduced to one Presbyterian denomination amongst several. Its recovery by the end of the century was due in no small measure to the leadership of Norman MacLeod.* He was called to be minister of the Barony Kirk, Glasgow in 1851...

The Barony, next to Glasgow Cathedral, had some of the worst slums of the city in its parish. In a flurry of activity, the energetic minister organized district meetings for adult education, founded the first Congregational Penny Savings Bank in Glasgow, set up a refreshment room where people could get cheap food, and established a reading room. New recreational facilities were organized, the mission staff of the church was increased from one to five, the congregation held parish missions, six new churches were created in the parish.

People crowded into the Barony to hear Norman preach. His biggest concern was that the poor were excluded because they didn't have proper clothes to wear or couldn't afford the seat rents; his solution was to hold special evening services at which people who were respectably dressed were turned away. Fourteen hundred people, all dressed in working clothes, regularly filled the church; and some of the people in the congregation were members of the Glasgow upper class who had dressed down for the occasion. Moleskins borrowed from their servants helped them to slum their way in.

from *George Macleod* by **Ronald Ferguson**

Norman MacLeod (1812–1872) was the grandfather of George MacLeod, founder of the Iona Community

102

Take me as I am —
that 'me' beneath an outer shell
so carefully contrived
for common use.

Take me as I am —
strip down these trimly fit veneers
conforming on my daily round
to what the world thinks
I should be.

Take me as I am —
and when you reach my core,
knowing then how far I'm short
of what I ought to be —
still take me.

Margaret Connor

103 *Love's Insight*

Take me, accept me, love me as I am;
Love me with my disordered wayward past;
Love me with all the lusts that hold me fast
In bonds of sensuality and shame.
Love me as flesh and blood, not the ideal
Which vainly you imagine me to be:
Love me, the mixed-up creature that you see;
Love not the man you dream of but the real.
And yet they err who say that love is blind.
Beneath my earthy, sordid self your love
Discerns capacities that rise above
The futile passions of my carnal mind.
Love is creative. Your love brings to birth
God's image in the earthiest of earth.

Robert Winnett

104 *Accept me*

Accept me as I am
and not as you would mould me;
I am not made
of your imagination and desire,
the fantasies
which veil us from each other;
I am what I am
woman and white,
carrying the genes and genesis
of countless generations,
bearing the wounds of journeying
and their healing,
my rucksack
packed with memories
uniquely mine.

Accept me
as I am learning
to accept myself,
help me uncover
the layers of unknowingness,
the pride and prejudice
conditioning
my view of you.
It requires a turning
towards each other,
steady gaze,
shared tears and laughter,
tenderised truth,
humility,
until the dawn breaks
in each other's eyes
and we know
that we are moulded
in the image of God.

Betty Hares

105 I sing a new Christ

I sing a new Christ, the joyful, merry guest,
Who fills with wine your empty cup,
Listens when song is your heart's pursuit,
He blesses the wedding, and its fruit,
All the children as they grow up.

I sing a new Christ, the hero of weekdays,
His halo of fine wood-fire spun
The one who from workshops builds a church
From cotter's laments makes psalms emerge
The Carpenter, the people's son.

I sing a new Christ, terror of profiteers,
His whip will bring wonders diffused
Who out of oppressed millions' sorrow
Will conjure a new Earth tomorrow
The Christ of the crushed and the abused.

Come, let us open wide like a mouldy barn
Christ's church that was almost a jail,
Scatter the seeds and spread his new Word
Till in all the sad hearts it is heard
In factory, meadow, hill, and dale.

Tibor Tollas
Translated from the Hungarian by Livia Var

Your will be done...

Think of a world that could be.

It could be...

Signs and symbols

Opening doors

Building the kingdom

Versions of the Lord's Prayer

The Revised Version Bible versions (1885)

The Revised Version is a revision of the Authorised Version

Our Father which art in heaven,
Hallowed be thy name.
Thy kingdom come.
Thy will be done,
as in heaven so on earth.
Give us this day our daily bread.
And forgive us our debts,
as we also have forgiven our debtors.
And bring us not into temptation,
but deliver us from the evil one.

Matthew 6. 9b – 13

Father,
Hallowed be thy name.
Thy kingdom come.
Give us day by day our daily bread.
And forgive us our sins;
for we ourselves also forgive every one that is indebted to us.
And bring us not into temptation.

Luke 11. 2b – 4

106 *Think of a world that could be*

It could be...

Think of a world that could be;
Too long have greed and hatred raged,
By our own hand the world is caged,
How can the Kingdom come?
Is harmony an idle dream,
Justice and mercy but a scheme
Only reserved for some?

Pray for a world that can be,
When self is routed from its lair
And love becomes the rightful heir —
Pray that this time will be ;
When all the earth is loved and shared,
Ravaged, polluted things repaired,
All creatures join the plea.

Work for a world that must be;
It's not enough to sit and hope,
Or dimly wish and blindly grope —
The dawn can speed the night.
The time is now — before too late,
Before we are destroyed by hate —
For love needs lamps to light.

Sing of a world that shall be;
Its rays of hope break through the gloom,
And now awaking from our tomb
We walk to meet the sun:
Transmuting wrong, as love has taught,
The Spirit's alchemy is wrought —
The will of God is done.

Cecily Taylor

Your will be done...

107 *creation*

No one will ever know
of the digging —
the words and the stones
thrown
the fallen trees
to heave
from the path
the boulders.

They will only see
the grown tree —
the birds that sing
in the space
of the branches;
hear the meaning of the leaves
in the curve of the song.

No one will ever know
how we climbed a third mile
and we
even we
shall forget —
and smile.

Cecily Taylor

108 Listen to the salutation of the dawn.
  Look to this day;
In its brief course lie all the verities
  and realities of our existence:
The bliss of growth, the glory of action,
  the splendour of beauty.
For every yesterday is but a dream
  and every tomorrow is only a vision
But today well lived
  makes every yesterday a dream of happiness
  and every tomorrow a vision of hope.
Look well, therefore, to this day,
For such is the salutation of the dawn.

A Hindu prayer

109 *Not only Abram and Sarah*

... there have been others also
in later days
who have pushed out a boat
not knowing where they were to go,
have left a shore of theories and prejudice,
scrambled over the shingle of their illusions,
and leapt aboard,
betting their life upon a ship of hope.

They have set their sails
against the gales of adversity
in such a way
that the sea which fought them
has also carried them onward:

and after the storms
there has been inexplicable peace within.

When the voyage was completed
it would have been difficult
for them to explain,
except to say:
By night there was the pole star to guide us,
and all the time
that mysterious magnetic pull
in the compass of the mind.

Cecily Taylor

110

The work of the priest

How beautiful will be the day
when all the baptised understand
that their work, their job,
is a priestly work,
that just as I celebrate Mass at this altar,
so each carpenter celebrates Mass at his workbench,
and each metal-worker,
each professional,
each doctor with the scalpel,
the market woman at her stand,
are performing a priestly office!
How many cabdrivers, I know, listen to this message
there in their cabs;
you are a priest at the wheel, my friend,
if you work with honesty,
consecrating that taxi of yours to God,
bearing a message of peace and love
to the passengers who ride in your cab.

Oscar Romero

111 Heart Question

On hearing a radio interview with a child in Bosnia
who had been injured by shell-fire. April 1994.

I heard you speaking,
simply, slowly,
and with worldly wisdom
wrought of shell-fire, sniper's sight,
and fear, and want —
and I wept.

I'd wept before you spoke,
tears for myself and life's frustrations.
But now, dear God!
how can this happen to a child
(old woman, newly wed)?

It happens through the choices people make.
The gentlest soul, it seems,
can brutalise what otherwise
is young and free.
And finer, purer things of flesh and blood
yield readily to powder blast and splintered steel.

I wonder now, how can it be,
your slow clear voice,
my tearful triviality,
commingle in some grand Divine economy
where damp and rust frustrate the killer's art,
and victory becomes, not steel, but heart?

Ian Fosten

Your will be done...

112 Choices...

Choices
that we make
help shape our ends
and yet the way we take,
one thing
dependent on another,
is often not
what we'd foreseen.

A fettered freedom
is the most
that we can hope to know,
and so within the bonds
of that constraint
may all our choices
then be wise,
with no complaint
if cherished schemes
are sometimes
cut to size.

Margaret Connor

113 Choices...

People often think of Christian morality as a kind of bargain in which God says, 'if you keep a lot of rules I'll reward you, and if you don't I'll do the other thing'. I do not think that is the best way of looking at it. I would much rather say that every time you make a choice you are turning the central part of you, the part that chooses, into something a little different than it was before. And taking your life as a whole, with all your innumerable choices, all your life you are slowly turning this central thing into either a heavenly creature or into a hellish creature.

C. S. Lewis

114 Choices...

The 'Our Father' compels us to recognise that we have a role in the world. To ask that His Kingdom may come while doing nothing to further the rule of love in the world is to mock God. Would it not make a mockery of ourselves, our brothers, and of God Himself if we were to ask for our daily bread without attempting — in our situation — to resolve the economic problems which we face in our country? Would it not also make a mockery of ourselves, our brothers and of God himself, if we were to ask to be delivered from evil and at the same time did not strive to develop our political and social institutions which provide the conditions for internal and external peace in the future?

R Coste

115 *Bounty*

In my pocket
I keep four jagged pieces
of coloured paper.
A child who has just learnt
to use scissors
gave them to me.

As I was leaving
he leant towards me
with the air of a Maharaja
bestowing half a kingdom.
'You have these now', he said,
'From me!'
And I treasure them
in equal measure.

Cecily Taylor

Signs and symbols

116 *Concentration*

Ilse, a childhood friend of mine, once found a raspberry in the camp, and carried it in her pocket all day to present it to me that night on a leaf. Imagine a world in which your entire possession is one raspberry, and you give it to a friend.

Gerde Weissman Klein, Holocaust survivor

117 *Keeping company with the fallen*

A child who was late in returning from an errand explained to her worried parents that she had come across a friend who had dropped her beloved china doll and it had smashed to pieces on the sidewalk. 'Oh,' her father said, 'you stopped to help her pick up the pieces.' 'No,' the child answered, 'I stopped to help her cry.'

Quoted in *High-Flying Geese* by Browne Barr

118 *Treasure*

My greatest richness this:
That little children bring me flowers.

A child sees beauty in the upturned glory of the flower
That gazes back at her to mirror shining purity.
She stretches out her hand in eager, swift response
To take the patterned beauty for her own,
Her answer here; that she has seen and loved.
> Perfect fulfilment for the flower is this,
> Her beauty loved and taken; as rich reward
> As that her beauty fades and falls,
> In the enrichment of the seed.

The spirit of the flower absorbed into the watching child,
Perfect perception in pure eyes of love,
Fulfilment for the child and flower.
> As gladly as she thus received them,
> (Eager young fingers snapping crisp young stem)
> She turns and gives them in her love to me.
Aware of the great gift bestowed,
I share the gift that beauty sowed.

My greatest richness this,
That little children bring me flowers.

Joan Brockelsby

119 *Beautiful*

I was walking in the park
I saw a flower
I said 'Hello'
The flower said 'Hello' back
We started to talk
'What are you doing today?'
Jason trod on the flower
It started to die
I went to see it
It was dead
I saw Jason
But he just walked away.

Marc Heslop, aged 10

120 *Touching*

A minister was once questioned about what appeared to be an excessive amount of body contact structured into the morning liturgy of his congregation. He replied, 'Our congregation, in this affluent neighborhood, includes an incredible number of divorced or otherwise single women, most of them trying to rear one or two children by themselves. They go from Sunday to Sunday without touching or being touched by anyone except their own children. At least here once a week some other human being touches them and acknowledges that they are persons, too, with hurts and needs.'

Browne Barr

121 *A new definition*

After being told six days of the week that they were nothings, by the rulers of white society, on the Sabbath, the first day of the week, black people went to church in order to experience another definition of their humanity.

James H. Cone

122

We believe in God
In Jesus Christ
In the Holy Spirit,
And in you and me.
We believe the Holy Spirit has freed us
To worship as a Community.
We believe the Holy Spirit works through
Balloons and ministers,
Daisies and wiggly children,
Clanging cymbals and silence,
Drama and the unexpected,
Choirs and banners,
Touching and praying,
Spontaneity and planning,
Faith and doubt,
Tears and laughter,
Leading and supporting,
Hugging and kneeling,
Dancing and stillness,
Applauding and giving,
Creativity and plodding,
Words and listening,
Holding and letting go,
Thank you and help me,
Scripture and alleluias,
Agonizing and celebrating,
Accepting and caring,
Through you and through me,
Through love,
We believe God's Holy Spirit lives
in this community of dancing, hand-holding
people where lines of age and politics and
lifestyles are crossed.
We believe in praising God for life.
We believe in responding to God's grace
and love and justice for all people.
We believe in the poetry within each of us.
We believe in dreams and visions.
We believe in old people running and children leading.
We believe in the Kingdom of God within us.
We believe in Love.

Anon

123 *Beautiful Attitudes*

You will be happy if you share your things or even give them away.
You will be happy if you are gentle and let others go first.
You will be happy if you cheer up those who are sad and lonely.
You will be happy if you stand up for what is right.
You will be happy if you forgive when people hurt you.
You will be happy if you are first to say sorry after a quarrel
     — even when you were right.
You will be happy if you don't try to get your own back if people laugh at you and make fun of you.
You will be happy if you think about our Father in heaven and often talk to him.

Source unknown

124 *Bless him, Lord Jesus*

A couple prayed for Stephen Lawrence as he lay dying, the inquiry was told. Conor Taaffe and his wife, Louise, who had just left a church meeting, stroked the 18–year-old's hair as he struggled to breathe. Mr. Taaffe, 32, told police: 'I was praying in a whisper, "Bless him, Lord Jesus, have mercy on him". '

He told the inquiry (yesterday) that his wife 'put her hands on his head for comfort, she spoke in his ear. I thought it was such a lovely thing for her to do. Both of us knew that the hearing was one of the last things to go, and she said, "You are loved, you are loved". '

Mr Taaffe said he believed that Stephen had died before he went to hospital and that even a surgeon on the scene could not have saved him.

He and his wife went to their nearby parish church to pray as the teenager was being taken to hospital. When Mr.Taaffe arrived home, he washed Stephen's blood from his hands into a container and poured the water under a rose bush in his garden. 'I thought in some ways perhaps he is living on a bit,' the advertising manager told the inquiry.

From a report in *The Times* 27 March 1998

125 *Sow me*

Sow me in the desert sands,
sow me on rock and stony ground,
sow me in thistle and thorn,
    for only when you sow me can I make the desert bloom,
    turn thorns into a holy crown, and rocks into a tomb.

Sow me in the market places,
sow me in hard and mocking hearts,
sow me in the prison and the pub,
    for only when you sow me can I make my loving real,
    bring peace instead of anger and hope instead of fear.

Sow me in the darkest night,
sow me in death and helpless tears,
sow me in the sickness and the pain,
    for only when you sow me can I bring a healing light,
    release the grieving spirit or give the blinded sight.

Sow me in your work and prayer,
sow me in all the ways you take,
sow me in the people that you meet,
    I need you to sow me whatever is around,
    for anyone can sow me in the good and fertile ground.

Colin Ferguson

126 *Founder of the Iona Community*

'I remember preaching individual salvation in the street in Govan one day — yes to 500 men on a weekday at 4 o'clock. What else was there for them to do in the market place but listen to curate or Communist? An outspoken man in question time, speaking almost as God spoke to Isaiah, asked: "Do you think all this religious stuff will save?" Very down at heel he was, but very clear of eye. Suddenly, as he was speaking, I realised he was preaching the gospel and not I. I asked him to come up on the platform, but he refused and left the meeting.

'Some weeks later I received a message asking me to go to hospital and see a man called Archie Gray. I had never heard the name before, but when I reached the hospital I found it was my questioner from the meeting and he was dying of starvation. The man was single, in a whole household of unemployed, which he had left because he felt he was eating too much of the rations. Out of 21 shillings a week he was sending 7/6 a week to a ne'er-do-well brother in Australia. He said he was bitter about the Church, not because it was preaching falsehoods, but because it was speaking the truth and did not mean what it said.

'Archie Gray was the true founder of the Iona Community.'

George MacLeod , founder of the Iona Community

127 *The meaning of socialism*

Socialism, in truth, consists, when finally resolved, not in getting at all, but in giving; not in being served, but in serving; not in selfishness, but in unselfishness; not in the desire to gain a place of bliss in this world for one's self and one's family (that is the individualist and capitalist aim), but in the desire to create an earthly paradise for all.

Bruce Glasier
From *The Meaning of Socialism* (1919)

128 The Door

Go and open the door.
Maybe there's a mountain glittering
with snow.
Maybe there's a fairground with
crowds of people.
Maybe there's a countryside, with birds
singing and trees whispering.
Who knows what you will see.

Go and open the door.
Maybe there's a fish tank with
different coloured fish to see.
Maybe there's a wedding with beautiful
bridesmaids and a beautiful bride
Or there's a volcano with red hot flame.
Who knows what you will see.

Go and open the door.
Maybe there's a land with lots of
beautiful creatures people never knew
were alive.
Maybe there's a cave with a monster
trying to get out.
Or a sky full of stars.
Who knows what you will see.

Joanne Openshaw, aged 11 years

129 *At the door*

When the sun is high and the house is full,
And the laughter is easy
And all is well —
Behold, I stand at the door and knock.

When the lights are low and the house is still,
And the talk is intense
And the air is full of wondering —
Behold, I stand at the door and knock.

When the lights are off and the house is sad,
And the voice is troubled
And nothing seems right —
Behold, I stand at the door and knock.

Come in, Lord Jesus, stay with us.
Bring to our house your poverty.
For then we shall be rich.

Bring to our house your pain
For then we may also share your joy.

Bring to our house your broken heart
That this may become a place of healing.

With friend, with stranger,
With neighbour and the unknown ones,
Be among us today.
For the doors of our house we open,
And the doors of our hearts we leave ajar.

Source unknown

130 *Wake up!*

It is time to wake out of sleep
Out of the shadows which haunt the past
    into the song lines
      which follow a star to a stable.

It is time to wake out of sleep
Out of the shadows which shape our dreams
    into the bread ways
      which follow a star to a table.

It is time to wake out of sleep
Out of the shadows which hedge us round
    into the hope paths
      which follow a star to a city.

It is time to wake out of sleep
Out of the shadows which hide your face
    into the rainbows
      which follow a star to a garden.

Betty Hares

131 *Divine Discontent?*

Father,
why are we such restless creatures,
so often longing for something different,
so often looking for happiness
beyond our present experience?

Is this restlessness evil
or is it a gift?
Might it come from you?
Could it be a divine discontent
which will never be satisfied
until we have discovered
the inner meaning of our lives?

Help us to ask the right questions
of our world
and of our own daily living;
and save us from being content
with inadequate answers.
Teach us the humility
of the truly wise
who know that the nearer they come
to the heart of the truth
the nearer they will be
to you.

Edmund Banyard

132 *The Ark*

Be thankful
he didn't build it in the cellar
where the vision
which became a boat
could not be sneered at.

Noah would have felt
a right twit
struggling to launch an ark
full of elephants and fleas
and the other paraphernalia
of creation
from the basement.

His hope was built
for all to see
and jeer at.
Nails, wood, ladders,
pots of pitch, brushes,
the clobber
of a boat-builder
preparing to float.

In the open
God flings his promise
across the sky
shouts
'I love you'
in the spangled curve
of sun through rain
which holds the earth
with a striped handle.

Felicity Prescott

Building the Kingdom

133 *New Life*

We will build a home in a new world,
    with the bricks of tolerance.
We will build a new world
    with the bricks of understanding,
We will build a new world
    with the bricks of hope,
We will build a new world
    with the bricks of community,
We will build a new world
    with the bricks of love,
We will build a new world
    with your people, Lord.
We will build a new world
    with your help.
We will build together a new world,
    where everyone will have a home
and where we will be part of one another
and part of you.
Through Jesus Christ our Lord.

Anon.

134 *Dog Days*

'When you stop to consider
The days spent dreaming of a future
And say then, that was my life.'

For the days are long —
From the first milk van
To the last shout in the night,
An eternity. But the weeks go by
Like birds; and the years, the years
Fly past anti-clockwise
Like clock hands in a bar mirror.

Derek Mahon

135 *Faith for Today*

We believe in God the Father,
who created all the world
who will unite all things in Christ
and who wants all his people to live together
as brothers and sisters in one family.

We believe in God the Son
who became man, died and rose in triumph
to reconcile all the world to God,
to break down every separating barrier
of race, culture or class,
and to unite all God's people into one body.
He is exalted as Lord over all,
the only Lord over every area of life.
He summons both the individual and society,
both the Church and the State,
to seek reconciliation and unity between all,
and justice and freedom for all.

We believe in God the Spirit,
the pledge of God's coming reign,
who gives the Church power
to proclaim the Good News to all the world,
to love and serve all people,
to strive for justice and peace,
to warn the individual and the nation of God's judgement,
and to summon them both to trust the Good News
and to obey Jesus Christ as King.

To God: Father, Son and Holy Spirit,
be glory, honour and power for ever and ever! Amen

The Presbyterian Church of Southern Africa, 1985

136 Building Community

We fall between the gaps we make.
Sometimes a bridge is built, but then,
Foundations insecure and planks worked loose,
It falls.

Youth and age; that gap is clear:
How often does the youth club meet
The luncheon club for mid-day pensioners,
Darby and Joan, the Toddlers' Mums?
> Yet will not one day
> All youth find greying hair and stumbling tread?
> And were not ancient ones a teenage crowd;
> Noisy, fancy-free, and locked within themselves?

Black and white,
Pink, brown and yellow,
Purple, if you please,
Or variegated crimson-blue.
Widen the gap! The colours are too bright!
> Yet shall we ever find the rainbow crock of gold,
> Without each other?

Men and women; women, men:
Uniting well in sex,
But not committees,
Unless they're pushed by mathematic rule
To find the statutory ones;
Create some fulcrum for uneasy balance.
> Yet who can tell which one the Spirit next will touch
> And truth engender?

A man once came, not quick to blame,
Not strident in his ways, but with God's truth ablaze;
More ready to be struck than strike.
The curtain tore in two,
And God met us, and Gentile, Jew.
A bridge was built,
And all the world was new.

But that was long ago.

Donald Hilton

137 One opinion?

Karl Barth stressed the transcendence, the 'otherness' of God, and the sinfulness of man. Man, he said, could not find God through natural religion, he could only know Him through His gracious revelation in Jesus Christ. 'Merely to talk about man in a loud voice is not to talk about God,' Barth insisted.

George was unimpressed by the Barthian separation of God from natural human life, muttering that 'Barth is easier to pronounce than to apply'. Two of Barth's most brilliant Scottish disciples were Thomas F. Torrance and J.K.S. Reid (who would both become prominent professors of theology) and both wrote to George in uncompromising terms, pointing out the error of his ways.

... George MacLeod's reply was equally uncompromising.

'To me, Christian orthodoxy is essentially a belief in a Person who always has many things to tell us but we cannot hear them now. He has given the Spirit of Truth that shall guide us into all the truth: a sentence that implies that we must keep moving. I really don't know what heresy is in these terms: though I can see how heresy can be defined if once orthodoxy is admitted as an intellectual set of formulae. If I wanted that I would go to Rome. I do not go there because the Roman Church seems to me the logical result of trying to 'pin down' orthodoxy. Short of Rome there is this mixty maxty business of many opinions: with your school trying to pin us down to 'one opinion' again and calling out all the others as the devil's agents. I'm glad your school keeps hammering at 'one opinion': keeps chucking in the spice which Barth said had been left out of the pudding too long. What makes me sad is the insistence that the entire pudding should be made of this spice: this calling out of all the others as the devil's agents.

From *George MacLeod* **by Ronald Ferguson**

138 On the Edge

Living on the edge of the church
I am tolerated,
patronized or even pitied
because I haven't seen the Light
and can't accept the Truth
of its teaching or tradition.
But the light can be a fire of love
or the blinding glare of a torture
    chamber.
The light of the church
has been both,
is both,
So I must choose
when to add my candle to that
    light;
And truth can be a liberation
or an imprisoning straight-jacket.
The truth of the church
has been both,
is both,
So I must choose
when to add my candle to that
    truth.

Living on the edge of the church
my candle is unseen,
the whisper of my truth unheard.
If my candle joins the others
to make a warmer glow
the church turns its face away.
If my whisper becomes a shout
the church closes its ears.
Are my light and truth
so frightening
that they must be rejected out of hand?
Are my questions so threatening
that they can't be entertained
for a moment?
Is the church so blind and deaf
that it can only see its own art,
hear only its own music?

How many bonfires must I light?
How many megaphones must I use?

Living on the edge of the church
is dangerous
for bonfires can rage
out of control
and megaphones deafen
or seem to blow my own trumpet.
Yet the light of truth
is a candle
which with other candles
dispels the dark
without destroying it;
And the whisper of truth
arises from the depths of wisdom
and is easy to miss
in the din of shouting.
If I can't make myself
seen or heard
without a raging fire
or a deafening shout
I risk destroying
what truth I have.

Living on the edge of the church
is dangerous
for if I draw near to the church
and my light is not seen
and my truth is not heard
I risk being absorbed
and buried with my truth
within the system of the church.
Then my candle no longer lights my way
and the whisper of my wisdom
no longer guides my step.

Living on the edge of the church
is lonely;
It would be easier
to surrender my mind
to its teaching and tradition.
I would then be accepted
and welcomed as a true son,
I want to be accepted
but I cannot live a lie:
I can only stand on the edge
until my whispering wisdom
can make itself heard
within the church.

Maybe the church will learn
to listen.
Maybe I shall learn
to speak
in a more penetrating whisper.
Until then
I must live my truth on the edge.

Peter Brice

139 A just society

'But back to justice. You said that Marx thought capitalism was an unjust form of society. How would you define a just society?'

'A moral philosopher called John Rawls attempted to say something about it with the following example: Imagine you were a member of a distinguished council whose task it was to make all the laws for a future society.'

'I wouldn't mind at all being on that council.'

'They are obliged to consider absolutely every detail, because as soon as they reach an agreement — and everybody has signed the laws — they will all drop dead.'

'Oh ...'

'But they will immediately come to life again in the society they have legislated for. The point is that they have no idea which *position* they will have in society.'

'Ah, I see.'

'That society would be a just society. It would have arisen among equals.'

'Men *and* women!'

'That goes without saying. None of them knew whether they would wake up as men or women. Since the odds are fifty-fifty, society would be just as attractive for women and for men.'

'It sounds promising.'

'So tell me, was the Europe of Karl Marx a society like that?'

'Absolutely not!'

Jostein Gaarder, from *Sophie's World*

Your will be done...

140 The Soapbox Rally

All morning we had worked,
enveloped in an atmosphere of promise,
constructed out of hope and summer dew,
and sun no longer warm but hot.

Selecting, sawing, assembling,
testing, and re-thinking,
dinner-time came so soon, too soon
for engineers intent upon development.

Likewise, the deadline for the race.
Our entry made it to the start,
dependent on its strength on nothing more secure
than string and some old blanket.

Surprise-less, then, we failed to reach
the bottom of the slope, but sat
as two contemplatives on sun-hot, Scout Hut driveway,
wreathed about by pram wheels, blanket, plank, and string.

At ten years old, you see,
there was so much we simply didn't know.

Ian Fosten

141 Trying

I made a picture in my head
To show me what life ought to be,
What it should give me.
But it didn't.

I made a picture by the proper rules
Taught me by society
By family and school and church,
Then took a rest
And waited for it all to happen.
But it didn't.

I think I am a lousy painter
Or a lazy one.
Is it too late to try again?

W. S. Beattie

142 *Stone-throwing*

A stone is thrown
into a calm lake
and the stone makes waves
spreading, reaching to the far end.

Let us throw stones
into a deadly calm lake
from all the edges of the lake
no matter how small is the stone
no matter how small is the wave.

The lake is like the world
The lake is like people's mind
The lake is like sisterhood
The lake is like human bondage
The lake is like chains of oppression

The stone brings awakening
The wave is a movement
And the movement spreads
when all of us
standing together on all sides
around the lake
keep throwing our little stones
The wave will never cease.

Till the whole lake
starts bubbling with life
Till the whole lake
makes its own spring
to keep its own life going.

Anon, Korea

Your will be done...

143 *Disturb us, Lord*

Disturb us, Lord, when we are too well pleased with ourselves,
When our dreams have come true because we dreamed too little,
When we arrive safely because we sailed too close to the shore.

Disturb us, Lord, when with the abundance of things we possess,
We have lost our thirst for the waters of life;
Having fallen in love with life, we have ceased to dream of eternity,
And in our efforts to build a new earth,
We have allowed our vision of the new Heaven to dim.

Disturb us, Lord, to dare more boldly,
To venture on wider seas, where storms will show your mastery;
Where, losing sight of land, we shall find the stars.
We ask you to push back the horizons of our hopes,
And push us in the future in strength, courage, hope, and love.

This we ask in the name of our Captain, who is Jesus Christ.

From St. James' Church, New York City

144 *Birth pangs*

Lord,
Help us to see in the groaning of creation
not death but birth pangs.
Help us to see in suffering
a promise for the future,
because it is a cry against the inhumanity of the present.
Help us to glimpse in protest
   the dawn of justice,
in the cross
   the pathway to resurrection,
and in desolation
   the seeds of joy.

Rubem Alves, Brazil

145 *Working for Unity*

Like branches of the vine, the Lord said,
we shall find our unity in him,
his word, his life, his cross, his spirit, his love.
Why then are good Christians so divided?
Are we not good Christians at all?

So I asked the bishop, Are you one with me?
and he said, I'm sorry, dear friend,
but the Anglican communion can only receive you
if it shuts an eye and uses Nelson's telescope.
I asked a cardinal, Are you one with me?
and he said, In the spirit, dear boy, but not in the body,
for discipline must be observed or we end in chaos.
I asked the Methodist chairman, Are you one with me?
and he said, Only too happy just so long as you keep
items 421 to 897 in the latest edition of the rule book.

So in my prayer I asked the Lord, Am I one with you?
The Lord said, Yes, you are one with me
in my sorrow, loneliness and frustration.
You are not yet one with me
in my joy, my glory and my crown.
    That is ahead, the fruit of the vine,
    The wine for the feast,
    The feast of the Lamb.
So hold on, like the branch, for God's sake.

Bernard Thorogood

146 *Say No to Ecumenism*

Say 'no' to ecumenism
if what they mean by ecumenism is
a laboratory for mutual admiration,
dissolving the riches of tradition
for a watered-down worship,
reducing faith to an amorphous lump
in a crucible of conformity.

Tell them that ecumenism is
the acid bite of argument and the boiling of heated debate,
the distillation of new elements in our search for understanding,
the creation of compound ways of doing mission together;
the opening of eyes and ears
in the explosion of our faith.

Tim Woods

147 *A Cry in the Wilderness*

When shall I ever be heard?
How many times shall I cry?
I need courage and confidence.

Am I not called
For the truth and for right?
To fight and win that warfare
In homes, church and community?

God expects me to be brave and true.
Is He not depending on me?
O, cry and cry for truth and right!
Why not I to say it?

Am I not called to be Esther today?
Am I not to be like Deborah?

Why not stand for truth and right?
Why afraid, why not gain courage and be brave to say it?
If it means dying for the truth then let it be so.
For me to live is Christ, to die is gain!

Women rise up and gain courage.
Be brave and true.
Set things right for God's Kingdom
Not for the church alone!

Why dream constructive ideas
And let them vanish like that morning dew?
Because of fear of the Pharisees and Sadducees
of our days.

Take Jesus, model of courage and authority.

Women, don't you know who you are?
God needs workers brave and true.

May he then depend on you?

Catherine Nkosi, Malawi

No Empty Phrases

Give us today our daily bread

So let us come and share what's given —
This foretaste of the bread of heaven.

A hungry world

The Lord's table

Versions of the Lord's Prayer

The New English Bible versions (1961)

Our Father in heaven,
thy name be hallowed;
thy kingdom come.
thy will be done
on earth as in heaven.
Give us today our daily bread.
Forgive us the wrong we have done,
as we have forgiven those who have wronged us.
And do not bring us to the test,
but save us from the evil one.

Matthew 6. 9b – 13

Father, thy name be hallowed;
thy kingdom come.
Give us each day our daily bread.
And forgive us our sins;
for we too forgive all who have done us wrong.
And do not bring us to the test.

Luke 11. 2b – 4

148 *Grandchildren*

A hungry world

With your eyes
the children of the world
are searching my face
asking me questions.

With your hands
the children of the world
hungry for bread
tug at my clothes.

With your trust
the children of the world
climb on my lap
seeking safe shelter.

With your arms
the children of the world
put theirs around me
pleading for justice.

Cecily Taylor

149 *Crisis Face*

'One cup of rice is all we can allow.'
The eyes look back in hunger and in pain,
Wide, deep brown eyes sunken beneath the brow
Pulled taut by famine and a world insane

The rip of water tearing through the plain
Leaves goats and people islanded on hills;
They come to fear the never ending rain
And curse the Lord who will not pay their bills.

Too rapidly the face of earth now fills
With myriad faces, each demanding 'Why
Do I not count?' Enormous crisis kills
Our understanding; need defeats supply.

The Buddha smiles; in him no tears I trace.
Stay with us Christ, we need your crisis face.

Bernard Thorogood

150 *Winners and Losers?*

Can news ever be good for everybody?
Can one win
without another losing?
Can one eat
without another going hungry?
Can one grow richer
without another growing poorer?
Surely if it is good for the warder
it is bad for the prisoner;
good for the Arab,
bad for the Jew;
good for the establishment,
bad for the revolution?

But what if all are losers,
longing to exchange defeat for victory?
Hungry,
needing to hear of a meal that satisfies?
Poor,
lacking the only things that matter?
Prisoners,
waiting to hear the order for their release?

What if all around the world
there are women and men
longing to hear of a state
where there is neither
Jew nor Arab,
black nor white,
male nor female,
establishment nor revolution?

How do you see it
as you try to read your paper
standing beside me in the crowded train,
thrust into unwilling neighbourliness?

Edmund Banyard

151 Just an ordinary man

Dedicated to Bob Geldoff

Just an ordinary man —
Scruffy at that,
Unshaven chin,
And a battered old hat;
He felt his giving worthless
And so it all began,
For he became a catalyst
That ordinary man.

There's a whole lot of treasure
Locked in people's hearts
That's the kind of place
Where a vision can start;
Where miracles of loving
Are multiplying bread —
With everybody joining in
The hungry can be fed,

Just an ordinary man
made us think again
On the cause of want,
And the famine of grain,
And does the world spend money
To do the best it can?
We'll go on asking questions like
That ordinary man.
We'll try to help remembering
That ordinary man.

Cecily Taylor

Give us today our daily bread

152 *Be guided by your hunger*

The sign outside the café said,
'Be guided by your hunger.'
We looked at each other, you and I,
picking up the parable,
thinking of the times
we had misread spiritual hunger
and had unsatisfactory meals,
The world, it seems, is full of diets,
should and shouldn't, do and don't,
accompanied by pressured sales talk.
At times it has been hard to know
how best to nurture the soul
and in an absence of decision,
our inner selves have starved.

'Be guided by your hunger.'
The truth is always simple,
For hunger itself is the guide,
the gift from God that seeks God.
It will turn us from food too weak for us,
and likewise from food too strong,
and bring us to what is right
for our present stage of development.

We will be guided by our hunger
and whatever tastes good to the soul,
will be the feast of God.

Joy Cowley
from Psalms Down-Under (Catholic Supplies [N.Z.] Ltd.)

153 *Beatitudes*

Blessed be you, harsh matter, barren soil, stubborn rock:
    you who yield only to violence
    you who force us to work if we would eat.

Blessed be you, perilous matter, violent sea, untameable passion:
    you who unless we fetter you will devour us.

Blessed be you, mighty matter, irresistible march of evolution, reality ever
        new-born:
    you who, by constantly shattering our mental categories,
force us to go ever further and further in our pursuit of truth.

Blessed be you, universal matter, immeasurable time, boundless ether,
triple abyss of stars and atoms and generations:
    you who by overflowing and dissolving our narrow standards of
        measurement
    reveal to us the dimensions of God.

Teilhard de Chardin

154 *Beatitudes for the hungry*

Blessed is he who comes in the name of the Lord.
Blessed are the parents
    with food and drink, from supermarket and daily work,
    bringing gifts of food for the table.
Blessed is the aid worker
    with sacks of grain and drills for water,
    bringing hope for a neglected people.
 Blessed is the priest behind the table
    with cup and plate, and godly prayer,
    bringing signs of the eternal within the passing moment.
Blessed is the child
    with innocence, vulnerability and charm,
    bringing questions and insight, stumbling and purpose.
Blessed is the politician
    with vision and plan, strategy and conviction,
    bringing burning justice and cool endeavour.
Blessed are all who come in the name of the Lord.

Donald Hilton

155 Invited Guests

Luke 14. 15–20

The feast was spread for all to see,
the host then summoned company;
successful, rich and satisfied
they made excuses — even lied.
    Lives filled with self, lives packed with pride
    — lives too full to let God inside!

The host then sent to scour each street
for those whom 'nice' folk never meet.
He welcomed poor and blind and lame;
those crushed, forgotten, trapped by shame.
    Lives needing healing, lives raw and sore —
    lives our God could make whole once more!

The summons spread across the land,
'til all the hungry were at hand;
the door then closed to leave outside
those rich, complacent, satisfied.
    Feast for the crushed, feast righting wrong —
    feast that shouts God's great justice song!

This feast's now spread for you and me,
if we'll accept God's company.
Christ summons us from near and far,
no matter who or where we are.
    Laid down his life, paid every cost —
    Wine and bread to revive the lost!

So let us come, and share what's given —
this foretaste of the feast of heaven —
respond, receive, and be made new
for all the things we're called to do.
    Receive God's gift, that we may all
    live our lives to announce God's call!

John Campbell

These verses may be sung to the tune *Sussex Carol*

156 *To be human*

Man was put on this earth,
    as scripture tells us,
not to leave things
    the way they were —
God created Adam
    and he put him
in the garden
    to take care of it -
man is supposed to transform
    his world
so that it bears
    a mark of his own intelligence
and his own art
    and his own concern,
because only if that is there
    can there be a Christian dimension
to all this.
    If the world is going to be Christianized
it automatically means to be humanized.

Bernard Cooke

Give us today our daily bread

157 *Come, Let us Celebrate*

Come,
Let us celebrate the supper of the Lord.
Let us make a huge loaf of bread
and let us bring abundant wine
like at the wedding of Cana.

Let the women not forget the salt.
Let the men bring along the yeast.
Let many guests come,
the lame, the blind, the crippled, the poor.

Come quickly.
Let us follow the recipe of the Lord.
All of us, let us knead the dough together
with our hands.
Let us see with joy
how the bread grows.

Because today
we celebrate
the meeting with the Lord.
Today we renew our commitment
to the Kingdom.
Nobody will stay hungry.

Elsa Tamez, Mexico

The Lord's Table

158 *Song of Communion*

Let's go to the corn patch
to the supper of the Lord.
Jesus Christ is inviting
to his harvest of love.
The cornfields shine
in the sunlight,
let's go to the supper
of communion.

from The Nicaraguan Campesino Mass

159 *Christmas Eve Snow*

From the grey storehouse
of a reticent heaven,
fragile blessings fall.

I open my mouth,
receptive to the manna
gifted suddenly.

I catch a wafer;
its coldness appals my tongue:
a stinging fraction.

I think of the sword
piercing the heart of Mary —
crib shadowed by cross.

Bethlehem, my mouth,
waiting for the mixed blessing
of tomorrow's bread.

Kate Compston

160 *The Singing Bread*

The singing bread,
The laughing wine;
What joyous ecstasy is mine.

The song is hushed...
The laughter stills...
The peace of Love flows where it wills.

June Plaice

161 The Table

The meals we shared
in different ways and places
on our journey,
have all been special, sacramental,
you might say.

This meal no less,
and infiltrated by
a prowling sense of
expectation — anxious, tense
yet eager,

longing for the
entry of a kingdom,
of God not men;
embodied in his look and knowing
quietness.

The talk turns sour;
'betrayal' is the word,
though, having said,
a smile as if was seen dawn breaking,
distantly.

The meal proceeds:
past liberation is
recalled, but now
weaves, patterned, into hope and future
seamlessly.

The plates are cleared,
the cups likewise, and lives
that we had led
are left as we step lightly into
the garden.

Ian Fosten

Give us today our daily bread

162 Eucharist

I have always found it difficult to celebrate the eucharist, or Holy Communion, or whatever we call it. How can we sit in beautiful big buildings, eating and drinking from silver plates and chalices, 'in remembrance of' Jesus, who presumably never owned a house or silver utensils? That was a question I used to ask my Sunday School teacher. I could never figure out just exactly what it was Jesus had died for, if this was the way we commemorated him. Wouldn't it be better to feed the hungry and heal the sick as he had done?

The eucharist is considered such a sacred rite that many women feel unworthy to partake of it during their period. In such a context, one can understand why some churches hesitate to ordain women as priests who would not only partake, but actually serve the sacraments. Is the eucharist no more than that — just a rite for which one has to attain a level of purity? Very exclusive?...

In Luke's version we get the impression that the context of the eucharist is the whole political problem of those who set themselves over against one another. Jesus' inviting his disciples to the Last Supper was a foretaste of the heavenly banquet, where such disputes should be no more, serving one another.

In the Church the eucharist should be the visible means of breaking through the socio-economic barriers, as it was in the life of the early Christians. Instead of accentuating such barriers, the Church should bring a eucharistic meaning to the broken life.

When women cannot serve the eucharist — when certain people feel ashamed because they cannot come to the table in the proper attire, when there is bickering about the ingredients to be used: may one use lime juice and cassava, or should one 'faithfully' stick to European bread and wine? — what is the eucharist then?

The eucharist is a sign. Instead of spending too much time polishing and upgrading the sign, perhaps Christians should reflect on what it stands for, and in which direction it is pointing. Whether it communicates inclusive or exclusive being.

As Father Tissa Balasuriya remarked, Jesus celebrated the eucharist only once, and within 48 hours he was dead, killed by the oppressive social structures he sought to liberate people from.

That is the true context of the eucharist.

Marianne Katoppo, Indonesia

Give us today our daily bread

163 When symbol and reality lose touch...

I have stopped offering mass, to live out the love for my neighbour in the temporal, economic and social orders. When my neighbour no longer has anything against me, and when the revolution has been completed, then I will offer mass again.

Camilo Torres. Roman Catholic priest and revolutionary, Colombia

164 The bread of death

At the beginning of the sixteenth century Bartolomeo de las Casas already saw the connection between a situation of exploited labour and the eucharist. A former slave-owner, he was ordained and prepared to celebrate the eucharist. He found this passage set for the reading:

If one sacrifices ill-gotten goods, the offering is blemished;
the gifts of the lawless are not acceptable.
The Most High is not pleased with the offerings of the ungodly,
    nor for a multitude of sacrifices does he forgive sins.
Like one who kills a son before his father's eyes
is the person who offers a sacrifice from the property of the poor.
The bread of the needy is the life of the poor;
whoever deprives them of it is a murderer.
To take away a neighbour's living is to commit murder;
    to deprive an employee of wages is to shed blood.

Sirach 34. 21–27

Hearing this stopped las Casas in his tracks. He abandoned the eucharist to return to Spain to get a charter for the Indians. He realised that the bread of the eucharist signifies not just the good earth, but also the human product, the fruit of exploited labour. Bread which is taken from the poor cannot be the bread of life, but is the bread of death. If we in the North are offering the fruit of the life of the poor at our eucharist we become like one who 'kills a son before his father's eyes'. Such an offering cannot be acceptable to the God and Father of our Lord Jesus Christ. It is only acceptable to the Moloch who loves to feast on human blood, and who demands human sacrifice. In that case our worship is not eucharist but idolatry, worship of Mammon.

Timothy Gorringe

165 *Anger, prayer and hope*

God of heaven and earth,
With gratitude we take this bread:
    symbol of the daily food which you provide
    to meet our needs.
With gratitude we take this wine:
    sign of gladness and rejoicing,
    symbol of celebration,
and offer both afresh to you,
within our sacrifice of praise.

With anger, Lord, we take this bread.
What is for us a sign of Christ
would be for some an emblem of their poverty.
For such a morsel some would fight:
    to ease their gnawing pain,
    to comfort a crying child,
    to hoard against tomorrow's disadvantage.

With anger, prayer and hope we take this bread
and drink this wine,
and offer of our work and time,
until the day of justice dawns,
when trade and gift, and plan and sacrifice,
produce a world that's worthy of your gifts,
and spreads its table over all the earth.

Donald Hilton

---

166 *Still we come*

Can we who every day
eat more than meets our need,
yet know of those
to whom bread is denied,
still come to this table
and take bread?

Can we, insulated in our ease,
and never visited by gnawing pains,
yet see and hear of those
daily assailed by hunger's grief,
still come to this table
and take bread?

Can we, who rest each night
in peaceful sleep,
tomorrow's menu clearly planned,
yet know the sleep of millions is disturbed
by pangs of hunger and by children's painful cries,
still come to this table
and take bread?

Can we, who come as beggars
to the table of the Lord,
yet know that others
in their begging for their daily bread
are Government-denied
and public-scorned,
and often too by us dismissed,
still come to this table
and take bread?

Yes, still we come,
and come we must:
to confess our part in others' loss;
to be challenged by the face of pain;
to feel the shame of inequality;
and to give thanks,
yes thanks,
that in our giving, prayers and work,
quick-born of love and love's demands,
we find a slender solidarity
with those who bear the burdens of time,
and meet them here, unseen,
the welcome guests of our own Lord.

Donald Hilton

Forgive us our sins, as we forgive...

I am sorry, Lord;
sorry to the very depths.

The fatal flaw

I have sinned

Sin incorporated

Versions of the Lord's Prayer

The Jerusalem Bible versions (1968)

Our Father in heaven,
may your name be held holy,
your kingdom come,
your will be done,
on earth as in heaven.
Give us today our daily bread.
And forgive us our debts,
as we have forgiven those who are in debt to us.
And do not put us to the test,
but save us from the evil one.

Matthew 6. 9b-13

Father, may your name be held holy,
your kingdom come;
give us each day our daily bread,
and forgive us our sins,
for we ourselves forgive each one who is in debt to us.
And do not put us to the test.

Luke 11. 2b-4

167 *Adam, where are you?*

The Fatal Flaw

No, I don't take any responsibility,
you see, Lord, I didn't actually
pick the apple, so I'm completely blameless.
No, Eve gave it to me
and obviously I didn't want to upset her;
girls like her are a bit few and far between.

Anyway she was only
responding to an invitation.
Yes, I know you said we weren't to
but it's not a matter of punishing us —
it was obviously the serpent's fault,
and when you've had time to mull it over
I'm sure you'll acknowledge
that you were the one
who put it in the garden
in the first place!

Cecily Taylor

168 *The Buck Stops...?*

'Don't blame me,' screamed Oppenheimer, carpenter of doom.
'My coffin's made to order, but I didn't draw the plans.
Don't blame me.'
'Well, don't blame me,' said Newton, in a mechanical voice,
'I only tell it as it is, pure and scientific, descriptive not prescriptive.
I didn't do it.'
'Neither did I,' cried Copernicus, revolving in his grave.
'Please don't blame me. My faith just needs understanding
of what turns the planets on.'
Plato sits above such squalid quarrels, contemplating beauty.
So it can't be his fault.
'And I am holy, perfect, sinless,' spake the Almighty.
'I am Creator,
but you can't blame me because I only create good things.
I am God.'
'Why not blame me?' said Eve. 'You usually do!'

Tim Presswood

169 Precaution

You know why
he turned both of them out
don't you?

Well, Adam would only
have started up
a logging company
in the primordial forest,
felling the Tree of Life
for mahogany toilet seats.

And Eve?
She would have taken over
the virgin beauty
of the shore-line,
promoted herself
to Managing Director
of Paradise Holidays Incorporated

and then
if not before
God would have been
turned out of Eden.

Cecily Taylor

170 Lowliness abused

'Tis a common proof,
That lowliness is young ambition's ladder,
Whereto the climber-upward turns his face;
But when he once obtains the upmost round,
He then unto the ladder turns his back,
Looks in the clouds, scorning the base degrees
By which he did ascend.

William Shakespeare
Julius Caesar Act 2. sc1

171 The Garden

Behind our memory
is the place we cannot remember
where we took form
and were at one
with that beyond ourselves.

Eden is a barren desert now
its sapling apple trees
are planted out into the world
to yield fruit after their kind,
as God intended it.

This Fall, this separation,
this state that we call sin
is not for lamentation and despair
nor for self-accusation.
God has not rejected us.
Does a mother reject the child she bears
when it leaves her body?

This world in which we live enclosed
will presently expel us
into a state that we cannot imagine
from earth's womb.

Yet do not be afraid
so Easter teaches us
compassionately.

The Garden is for hope and trust
whether it be Eden
or Gethsemane

W. S. Beattie

172 M.C.P.

The woman tempted me,
Said Adam, and I fell.
Had she not been so kind
I would have had to do it all myself
And take the blame. Don't tell,
Not Eve, nor anybody,
But it's worked out rather well.

W. S. Beattie

173 Sorry

I am sorry, Lord;
sorry to the very depths.
Sorry to that place where
my life and flesh,
and mind and spirit
meet and join
as one,
and make me
who I am.

I hope, Lord;
hope to the very heights.
Hope to that place where
your grace and love,
and steadfast mercy
meet and join,
that I may know you
as you are
and find my peace.

Donald Hilton

174 *ever more naked*

after the flood
Noah lived always in the tension
between the promise of the rainbow
and the memory of the choking screams
in the water, the scratching and sliding
of finger nails on the lurching sides
of his Ark.

in the bottle he found some resolution
he drowned the screams again
in an hour or two of forgetfulness, his eyes turned to the earth.

they found him naked and oblivious.
some things within him had not survived
the flood. Some things that did survive
already undermined his pretensions
to a brave new world.

We, his grandchildren, continue his work,
building ever more sumptuous illusions
to drown our struggling awareness

year by year
we are found ever more
naked.

Andrew M. Rudd

175 There is so much good in the worst of us,
And so much bad in the best of us,
That it hardly becomes any of us
To talk about the rest of us.

Anon

176 A Dream of Nature

Birds I saw in bushes made nests.
Even a simple one no man
Could ever make. And when and where
I wondered did the magpie learn
To weave sticks one with another
To secure her nest? Carpenters
Couldn't do anything as good,
No designer make a blueprint
For it either. It astonished
Me even more that many birds
Hid their eggs, carefully concealed,
So that only the parent birds
Themselves could find them. Some I saw
Did their breeding high in the trees
And hatched their young way up above
The ground. Diving birds plumped deep down
In swamps, moorland ponds and reedbeds
Wherever there was water. 'Dear
God,' I cried, 'What school do all these
Wild things go to, to get such sense?'
And then the peacock; I saw how
He mated, how roughly the bird
Went about it. I marvelled at
His splendour along with his crude
Screaming voice. I looked at the sea
And on further to the high stars.
The whole world was full of wonders
Too many to put down now, flowers
In the fields, their dazzling colours,
So many different shades, sprung
From the same earth and grassy fields,
Some bitter to the taste, some sweet.
It seemed all one great miracle
Ranged too wide for me to record.
But what struck me and set me back
Was that reason seemed to govern
All creatures and how they acted
Except for man, except for mankind.

William Langland (14th century)
from *The Vision of Piers Plowman*

177 *Forgive*

I cannot blame you,
For your eyes are bound by flesh like mine.
You are my fellow-mortal.
Have I to blame myself?
Or is it the human words,
the word that speaks what must be done,
Forgive?

Will you consent to be forgiven?
Will I consent?
Death and the Law say no,
But life speaks otherwise.

Life says, now
Not just two thousand years ago, but now
You shall forgive
And trust to be forgiven,
Yet with no mental note
'Though I forgave you once
I'll never trust you afterwards',
Nor even, 'Well, we'll speak no more
About it, but forget, and carry on
With what comes next'.

These leave a bruise that's slow to heal.
Such shadows have themselves to be forgiven
While the spear twists within the wound,
And Christ hangs still upon his cross.

Forgiveness is a reckless act whose folly is divine,
A simple ordinary thing that happens every day,
As hard and far more precious than the finest diamond:
Forgiveness is divine humanity.

W. S. Beattie

178 Wagtail and Baby

A baby watched a ford, whereto
　A wagtail came for drinking;
A blaring bull went wading through.
The wagtail showed no shrinking.

A stallion splashed his way across,
　The birdie nearly sinking;
He gave his plumes a twitch and toss,
　And held his own unblinking.

Next saw the baby round the spot
　A mongrel slowly slinking;
The wagtail gazed, but faltered not
　In dip and sip and prinking.

A perfect gentleman then neared;
　The wagtail, in a winking,
With terror rose and disappeared;
　The baby fell a-thinking.

Thomas Hardy

179 *Easter Imperfect*

Do you regret, Lord, coming back
from death to life in this imperfect world?
The tomb was quiet, peaceful, past
all fear and fret, past pain, remorse, regret,
a blessed blank beyond the chance of hurt.

They didn't even know you, even those
who claimed to love you most — two on the road
to Emmaus, Mary weeping in the garden ...
though Judas knew he couldn't believe it true
a man who killed his God could hope for pardon.

No man has greater love — you said yourself —
dares die for friends; but was it worth it?
Perhaps it takes more courage to return
here where we still must learn to hate and kill,
piling our pain on your intolerable burden.

And are you glad, Lord, coming back to find
refinements or advanced technology
enabling Cain to slay a million times —
science plus skill converts to overkill —
blasting men's lives and national economies.

So after death your disappointment must
be sharp and bitter. Can you now forgive
our violence to men and apathy towards you —
our love of pelf and even more of self?
Lord, you chose life — now teach us how to live!

Kenneth Wadsworth

180 *Peccavi*

I have sinned

I have sinned
Father, forgive me...

I have sinned
   I have looked on the world
     about me
   and been bored
   I have felt the sun on my face
   the west wind, rain
   and seen nothing wonderful
   I have eaten my daily bread,
     new-baked
   and felt no gratitude
Father, forgive...

I have sinned
   I have played doubting Thomas
   have doubted the words of love;
   I have doubted whether
     anything
   could be worthwhile
   I have doubted
   even my disbelief
Father, forgive...

I have sinned
   I have misused my time
   have failed to use gifts of hand,
     mind
   I have resented others' abilities,
     skill, success
   have been quick to blame
   I have buried my talent in the
     ground
   and my shame
Father, forgive...

Kenneth Wadsworth

I have sinned
I have seen swollen-bellied children
   too weak to swat the flies on
     weary eyelids;
   I have watched tv pictures of
     mutilated bodies
   I have walked past sleepers in
     cardboard boxes
   I have said: What a pity!
Father, forgive...

I have sinned
I have taken myself very seriously
have called myself chief of sinners
I have occupied the penitent's
   stool
the psychiatrist's couch.
I have examined my soul
have found it interesting, appalling
   absorbing
I have set myself firmly in the
   centre
And filled the periphery with my
   reflection.
I have... I
I... I... I... I
Father, forgive...

I have sinned.
Father, forgive me
live me.

181 *Adam is me*

There in a garden, when God called my name
I could not face him because of my shame.
Trust I had broken, I ate from his tree.
God forgive Adam, for Adam is me.

There in a garden Christ knelt down in prayer,
I helped them find him and I led them there.
They took him and killed him on Calvary's tree.
God forgive Judas, for Judas is me.

There in a courtyard, as Jesus was tried
I do not know him — three times I replied
there as a cock crowed was my treachery.
God forgive Peter, for Peter is me.

There in a garden he rose from his tomb,
When we were hiding he entered my room.
Doubt not my living, my wounds you can see.
God forgive Thomas, for Thomas is me.

Now in my life Lord, in my every day
I need your guidance to show me your way.
Faithless and fearful no more let me be
Be my forgiveness and come alive in me.

Colin Ferguson

182 The Sifting* of Peter

In St. Luke's Gospel we are told
How Peter in the days of old
    Was sifted;
And now, though ages intervene,
Sin is the same, while time and scene
    Are shifted,

Satan desires us, great and small,
As wheat, to sift us, and we all
    Are tempted;
Not one, however rich and great,
is by station or estate
    Exempted.

No house so safely guarded is
But he, by some device of his,
    Can enter;
No heart hath armour so complete
But he can pierce with arrows fleet
    Its centre.

For all at last the cock will crow
Who hear the warning voice, but go
    Unheeding,
Till thrice and more they have
          denied
The Man of Sorrows, crucified
    And bleeding.

One look of that pale suffering face
Will make us feel a deep disgrace
    Of weakness;
We shall be sifted till the strength
Of self-conceit be changed at length
    To meekness.

Wounds of the soul, though healed,
          will ache,
The reddening scars remain, and
          make
    Confession;
Lost innocence returns no more;
We are not what we were before
    Transgression.

But noble souls, through dust and heat,
Rise from disaster and defeat
    The stronger,
And conscious still of the Divine
Within them, lie on earth supine
    No longer.

Henry Wadsworth Longfellow

'Simon, Simon, listen! Satan has demanded to sift all of you like wheat.'
Luke 23.31

183 *Peter and Judas*

Could you not stay awake with me one hour?

Father, the sleep of Peter falls also on our unwilling eyes:
the hungry suffer and we sleep,
the lonely cry out in despair and we sleep,
the homeless grieve,
the workless are discounted,
the dying lose hope,
cities are burnt, communities destroyed,
and children die before they live,
and we sleep.
Father, forgive.

Would you betray the Son of Man with a kiss?

Father, the kiss of Judas is on our lips:
our words adore you but our lives deny
our worship honours you but has no root in love,
we make gestures of love but only to serve our selfish purpose.
Father, forgive.

Donald Hilton

184

Mine! says the child clutching
the toy which shatters, hacks
his small tight hand leaving
sobbing distress, pain, fear.

Mine! says the lover holding
soft flesh which shudders, grows
wrinkled and slack, betrays or
is betrayed by lust, time, death.

Mine! says the mother hugging
babe at the breast, vainly
protecting the growing person
against destiny, life, self.

Mine! says the merchant counting
commodities, profits, or
tramping his new estates, faces
of rivals who'll hail his bankruptcy.

Mine! says the painter, poet
swelling and shrunk with pride
in creating what the critic,
neglect or rust destroys, loses,
damns.

Yours! says God only who
contains reality entire, gives
self all utterly, withholding
nothing — to be yours, mine, his.

Kenneth Wadsworth

185 Into your hands

O, Lord,
Your hands once shattered
by crude, cruel nails
reached out for mine,
ready to receive failings and failures;
in a world
that I tried to understand,
that I tried to control.
But couldn't.
I commend my spirit.

Your hands so scarred
held mine so softly,
binding together
the broken pieces of myself;
of a life
that was no longer filled with hope,
that was no longer an expression of love.
But could be,
For you have redeemed me.

Living, loving hands,
consoled and cleansed
as they bathe me in your Holy Spirit;
and in that moment
the pain and sorrow of yesterday,
the hopes and fears of tomorrow,
were transfigured
by your precious, perfect grace.

Julia Bebbington

186 *Thee, God, I come from, to thee go*

Thee, God, I come from, to thee go
All day long I like a fountain flow
From thy hand out, swayed about
Mote-like in thy mighty glow.

What I know of thee I bless,
As acknowledging thy stress
On my being and as seeing
Something of thy holiness.

Once I turned from thee and hid,
Bound on what thou hadst forbid;
Sow the wind I would; I sinned:
I repent of what I did.

Bad I am, but yet thy child.
Father, be thou reconciled.
Spare thou me, since I see
With thy might that thou art mild.

I have life left with me still
And thy purpose to fulfil;
Yea a debt to pay thee yet:
Help me, sir, and so I will.

But thou bidst, and just thou art,
Me show mercy from my heart
Toward my brother, every other
Man, my mate and counterpart.

Gerard Manley Hopkins

187 Failure

What is wrong with failure?
A glorious failure
I mean, to fail well
Means you've got to put in tremendous effort in the first place,
And having gone to all this effort and trouble
Look at what you've learned,
What experience you have gained,
What knowledge from trial and error you have,
How very much further on you are,
Than if you had never ventured — and thus risked failure.

And now that calamity and collapse have blessed your venture,
You're still in one piece,
Been through the storm
More knowledgeable, more calm, more humble,
More mature and likely to succeed next time —
And maybe you will have learned something about faith.

Source unknown

188

Failure doesn't mean you have accomplished nothing:
It means you have learned something.
Failure doesn't mean that you have been a fool:
It means you have a lot of faith.
Failure doesn't mean you have been disgraced:
It means you were willing to try.
Failure doesn't mean you don't have it:
It means you have to do something in a different way.
Failure doesn't mean you are inferior:
It means you are not perfect.
Failure doesn't mean you have wasted your life:
It means you have a reason to start afresh.
Failure doesn't mean you should give up:
It means you must try harder.
Failure doesn't mean that you will never make it:
It means it will take a little longer.
Failure doesn't mean that God has abandoned you:
It means that God has a better way.

Anon

189 Just Suppose

Suppose we're not a fallen people at all,
but a people on the way up;
not caterpillars that once were butterflies,
but actually the other way round.

Just suppose we have this wonderful God
who is so much in love with us,
He has drawn us out of the animal kingdom,
giving us the divine spark of His love
to grow into a fire within us and eventually
bring us to oneness with Him.

Just suppose this wonderful God
so totally, crazily in love with us,
first becomes one with His beloved,
taking on a human likeness
to join us in our growing pains,
suffering everything we might suffer,
to show us the truth of the empty chrysalis.

And just suppose that our words of fear
like disobedience and judgement and condemnation,
belong not to a God who is total Love
but to a half-grown people
trying to explain their incompleteness,

Suppose that the only ultimate truth
is that God is the source
and destiny of every soul.
Suppose that everything we are,
all our light and shade, our sin and celebration,
belongs wholly in God's love.
Suppose no one is ever lost to that love.

Wouldn't that be Good News?

Joy Cowley
from *Aotearoa Psalms* **(Catholic Supplies [N.Z.] Ltd.)**

Forgive us our sins, as we forgive...

Sin Incorporated

190 Robbed Innocence

Amidst the tension of
the night-time hours
of war time
our children come of age;
they lose
their childhood.

Each blood-soaked body
destroys
their beautiful dawn
which soared like a bird.
Walls crack open
at the sound
of their childish laughter,

A burst of gunfire
from an automatic weapon
shatters the silence
of the star-lit night.
The meanings of fairy stories
fall dead

Shivaramani, Malaysia

They learn
to shut the gates early.
They learn to discern
the subtle differences
in the sound of dogs barking
in the village.
They learn to remain silent,
without asking questions.
They learn to remain silent
when there are no answers to their
            questions.
They learn to accept
whatever situation confronts them.
In fun
they tear the wings off
a captured dragonfly.
They play at war
with bits of stick
for guns.
As they play,
they kill each other
laughing.

191 *Betrayal*

We betrayed the poor, — we, the elite,
We, the fifteen out of every hundred,
Rose by ascending spirals to giddy heights,
While they, the eighty-five in every hundred,
Remained on earth, hungry.
We, the intelligentsia, betrayed the poor, for thirty long years.
We slept, we hibernated, while they toiled.

We thought only of the towel and the basin
And never of the toils of the revolutionary.
We failed to see their bleeding points.
We, the intellectuals, betrayed the cause.
We tasted the joys of life,
Amidst their joyless world of sweat and blood.

We planned, but no one planned the planners.
Our ideologies, our paths —
Sarodaya, Socialism, Secularism, Swatantra.
We forgot that ideologies are anthropologies —
hopes about man's nature and destiny.

We are nothing but hypocrites — cowards all,
Who call for sacrifice and selfless service, save for ourselves!

So again we are on square one,
To start the pilgrimage again.
Rich with hopes, heavy with anxieties,
Carrying with us the load of promises and threats.
'A journey of a thousand miles begins with the first step.'
Make this the first step, Lord,
And help us grasp the moment.
For your sake
And for the sake of six hundred million of your people.

Mathai Zachariah, India

Forgive us our sins, as we forgive...

192 Muted Cry

written in the late 1930's in the Philippines when the indigenous language was discouraged and English enforced as the language of literature.

They took away the language of my blood,
giving me one 'more widely understood.'
   More widely understood! Now lips can never
   Never with the Soul-in-Me commune:
   Moments there are I strain, but futile ever,
   To flute my feelings through some native Tune ...
Alas, how can I interpret my Mood?
They took away the language of my blood.
If I could speak the language of my blood
   My voice would whirl up through resistless space
   Swiftly — sure — flight no one can retrace,
And flung against the skyey breast of God,
   Its scattered words, charged with a passion rare,
   With treble glow would dim the stars now there.

   Shakespeare, Dante, Sappho, and the rest,
   They who now as poets deified.
Never their language being them denied,
Their moods could be felicitous expressed —
   Crimson of joy, purple of grief,
   Grey of unrest, white of relief,
Their dreams so coloured, living forms they seem,
The real lent enchantment like some faery-dream.
   If I could speak the language of my blood,
   My feet would trace the path their feet have trod,
   And stake me a niche within their lot of Fame,
   of jade-and-gold, and carve me there a name.
Ah, could I speak the language of my blood,
   I, too, would free the poetry in me
   And this now apathetic world would be
Awakened, startled at the silver flood
   Of Song, my soul aptly expressing,
   Each flood-note listeners impressing,
More as the water-drop into a pearl congealed
Than as a ripple on the ocean's breast revealed.

These words I speak are out of pitch with ME!
That other Voice? — Cease longing to be free!
   How can't thou speak who has affinity
   Only with promised-but-unflowered days,
   Only with ill-conceived eternity.
   Being, as they, mere space lost unto Space?
Forever shalt thou cry, a muted god:
'Could I but speak the language of my blood!'

An anonymous Filipino woman

193 *Nunc Dimittis*

written after the signing of the Israeli /Palestinian peace agreement in Washington, September 13th 1993.

He was old, dirty, half blind,
always haunting the synagogue porch,
moaning softly as he rocked:
'Lord, how long?'

Never into politics,
he'd been stoned selling papers
near the Western Wall.
Hit on the head, the Intifada
had left him addled
but harmless.

Smart young Jews stepped round him,
carefully upwind,
and threw a shekel or two
as he held out trembling arms
waiting to cradle hope for the world.
'Lord, how long — how long?'

One morning they found him
dead on the steps — stiff fingers
clutching a copy of the day's edition.
A picture showed
an Arab and Jew shaking hands.

When the Red Crescent orderly
brought a cover
to place on the slowly marbling face
he saw
the look of unutterable peace.

Margaret Connor

Forgive us our sins, as we forgive...

194 Forbidden Questions

Easter is better than Christmas because Dad takes us to the Redemptorist church where all the priests wear white and sing. They're happy because Our Lord is in heaven. I ask dad if the baby in the crib is dead and he says, No, He was thirty-three when He died and there He is, hanging on the cross. I don't understand how He grew up so fast that He's there with a hat made of thorns and blood everywhere, dripping from His head, His hands, His feet, and a big hole near His belly.

Dad says I'll understand when I grow up. He tells me that all the time now and I want to be big like him so that I can understand everything. It must be lovely to wake up in the morning and understand everything. I wish I could be like all the big people in the church, standing and kneeling and praying and understanding everything.

At the Mass people go up to the altar and the priest puts something into their mouths. They come back to their seats with their heads down, their mouths moving. Malachy says he's hungry and he wants some, too. Dad says, Shush, that's Holy Communion, the body and blood of Our Lord.

But, Dad.

Shush, it's a mystery.

There's no use asking more questions. If you ask a question they tell you it's a mystery, you'll understand when you grow up, be a good boy, ask your mother, ask your father, for the love o' Jesus leave me alone, go out and play.

Frank McCourt
From *Angela's Ashes*

195 The Non-Believer

Jesus was once taken to a football match. At the first goal he cheered wildly and threw his hat in the air. When the other side equalized, he again went wild with delight. A man behind him asked, 'Which side are you on?'
'Neither.' he replied, 'I'm just enjoying the game.'
'What are you?' the man asked. 'An atheist or something?'

Anon

196 *When the Tourists flew in*

The Finance Minister said
'It will boost the Economy
The dollars will flow in.'

The Interior Minister said
'It will provide full
and varied employment
for all the indigenes.'

The Minister of Culture said
'It will enrich our life ...
contact with other cultures
must surely
improve the texture of living.'

The man from the Hilton said
'We will make you a second
Paradise;
for you is the dawn
of a glorious new beginning!'

When the tourists flew in
our island people metamorphosed
into a grotesque carnival
a two week side-show

When the tourists flew in
our men put aside
their fishing nets
to become waiters
our women became whores

When the tourists flew in
what culture we had flew out of the
window
we traded our customs
for sunglasses and pop
we turned sacred ceremonies
into ten-cent peep shows

When the tourists flew in
local food became scarce
prices went up
but our wages stayed low

When the tourists flew in
we could no longer
go down to our beaches
the hotel manager said
'Natives defile the sea-shore.'

When the tourists flew in
the hunger and the squalor
were preserved as a passing
pageant for
clicking cameras — a chic eye-sore!

When the tourists flew in
we were asked to be 'side walk
ambassadors'
to stay smiling and polite
to always guide the 'lost' visitor...

Hell, if we could only tell them
Where we really want them to go!

Cecil Rajendra

197 *Amazing Grace*

Exceedingly odd
Is the means by which God
Has provided our path to the heavenly shore:
Of the girls from whose line
The true light was to shine
There was one an adulteress, one was a whore.
There was Tamar who bore —
What we all should deplore —
A fine pair of twins to her father-in-law;
And Rahab the harlot,
Her sins were as scarlet,
As red as the thread which she hung from the door;
Yet alone of her nation
She came to salvation,
And lived to be mother of Boaz of yore;
And he married Ruth,
A Gentile uncouth,
In a manner quite counter to biblical lore;
And of her there did spring
Blessed David the King,
Who walked in his palace one evening, and saw
The wife of Uriah,
From whom he did sire
A baby that died, oh, and princes a score.
And a mother unmarried
It was too that carried
God's son, and him laid in a cradle of straw,
That the moral might wait
At the heavenly gate
While the sinners and publicans go in before,
Who have *not* earned their place
But received it by grace,
And have found them a righteousness not of the Law.

Michael D Goulder

198 *No vice so simple*

So may the outward shows be least themselves.
The world is still deceived with ornament.
In law, what plea so tainted and corrupt
But, being seasoned with a gracious voice,
Obscures the show of evil? In religion,
What damnèd error but some sober brow
Will bless it and approve it with a text,
Hiding the grossness with fair ornament?
There is no vice so simple but assumes
Some mark of virtue on his outward parts.

William Shakespeare
The Merchant of Venice Act 3, Sc. 2

199 *Shared guilt*

'Tis one thing to be tempted, Escalus,
Another thing to fall. I not deny,
The jury passing on the prisoner's life
May in the sworn twelve have a thief or two
Guiltier than him they try.

William Shakespeare
Measure for Measure Act 2, Sc.1

200 *The Quality of Mercy*

The quality of mercy is not strained.
It droppeth as the gentle rain from heaven
Upon the place beneath. It is twice blest:
It blesseth him that gives, and him that takes:
'Tis mightiest in the mightiest. It becomes
The thronèd monarch better than his crown.
His sceptre shows the force of temporal power,
The attribute to awe and majesty,
Wherein doth sit the dread and fear of kings;
But mercy is above this sceptred sway.
It is enthronèd in the hearts of kings;
It is an attribute to God himself,
And earthly power doth then show likest God's
When mercy seasons justice.

William Shakespeare
The Merchant of Venice Act 4, Sc.1

Forgive us our sins, as we forgive...

Forgiving and Forgiven

201 The only child

I was six years old when I awoke to the reality of racism: from the sheltered environment of my home, I was pushed out into the world — a local elementary school just down the road from our house. I went there only for a month before city laws mandated that I be bussed across town to another school. My parents were not happy with this; they wanted me to go to a school where I was known and loved. They owned a farm out in the country, and so we moved there...

My father, a veteran of the civil rights movement, taught us love and respect for everyone — white or black. I did not see along racial lines. All the same, I was the only black child in the school, and many of the other children had obviously been taught to hate. Children can be brutal about each other's differences. They may begin with an innocent question: why is your skin brown? But then they start to laugh and mock, because they know that brown skin is somehow different; somewhere along the line they have been taught that it isn't 'normal'.

I felt out of place. I was a fish out of water, and these kids didn't make it easy for me. I introduced one of my white friends to another white kid on the bus one day, and from then on they always sat together but left me out.

Then when I was in the seventh grade in the city, there was a white guy in my class, Shawn, the only white in the whole school. We treated him as an outcast and taunted him with racial epithets and physically abused him. We took out our hatred of white people on him even though he hadn't done anything to harm any of us. We were angry. He symbolised everything that we knew about white people and their history: the humiliation of our people, the lynchings, the mobs, and the slave trade. We took out all our bitterness and anger on this guy.

I can see now that what we did to Shawn was wrong. We were racist, the very thing we despised whites for. Still today I ask for forgiveness for the harm I caused him. And I resolve to forgive the guys who didn't have the heart to love me when I was the only black kid in their midst.

Johann Christoph Arnold, quoting Jared, Boston U.SA. in *The Lost Art of Forgiving*

202 *Choice*

We choose to sin, holy, loving God,
we choose, we freely choose,
and that is the folly of it,
the folly and the terror.

And you choose to forgive,
you choose, you freely choose,
and that is the wonder of it,
the wonder and the joy.

Just one sign of repentance,
one hint of true penitence
that touches heart, mind, and soul,
body, life, and hope,
and you forgive;
and we, still prone to fail and fall
are glad;
glad of you
for being who you are.

Donald Hilton

203 *The cure*

Nothing is finished,
nothing is lost,
nothing is to be regretted.
All is grace,
all can be saved, all can be redeemed.
The blind see, the deaf hear,
the lame walk, the lepers are healed,
the dead are raised.
Through all these signs, God tells us:
'I who can cure the body and recreate it
can also cure your soul and recreate it.
Little person,
I can remake you,
create you anew.'

Henri Bouland

204 The long perspective of forgiveness

The hedgerows were deep and ragged where he walked, covered with the lace of cow parsley. The air had a feeling of purity as though it had never been breathed; it was just starting to be cool with the first breeze of the evening. From the tall elms he could see at the end of the field there was a sound of rooks, and a gentler calling of wood pigeons close at hand. He stopped, and leaned against a gate. The quietness of the world about him seemed to stand outside time; there was no human voice to place it.

Above him he saw the white moon, early and low above the elms. Over and beyond it were long jagged wisps of cloud that ran in ribbed lines back into the pale blue of the sky, then trailed away in gestures of vaporous white.

Stephen felt himself overtaken by a climactic surge of feeling. It frightened him because he thought it would have some physical issue, in spasms or bleeding or death. Then he saw that what he felt was not an assault but a passionate affinity. It was for the rough field running down to the trees and for the path going back into the village where he could see the tower of the church: these and the forgiving distance of the sky were not separate, but part of one creation, and he too, still by any sane judgement a young man, by the repeated tiny pulsing of his blood, was one with them. He looked up and saw the sky as it would be trailed with stars under darkness, the crawling nebulae and smudged lights of infinite distance: these were not different worlds, it seemed now clear to him, but bound through the mind of creation to the shredded white clouds, the unbreathed air of May, to the soil that lay beneath the damp grass at his feet. He held tightly on to the stile and laid his head in his arms, in some residual fear that the force of binding love he felt would sweep him from the earth. He wanted to stretch out his arms and enfold in them the fields, the sky, the elms with their sounding birds; he wanted to hold them with the unending forgiveness of a father to his prodigal, errant but beloved son. Isabelle and the cruel dead of the war; his lost mother, his friend Weir: nothing was immoral or beyond redemption, all could be brought together, understood in the long perspective of forgiveness. As he clung to the wood, he wanted also to be forgiven for all he had done; he longed for the unity of the world's creation to melt his sins and anger, because his soul was joined to it. His body shook with the passion of the love that had found him, from which he had been exiled in the blood and the flesh of long killing.

He lifted his head, and found that he was smiling.

Sebastian Faulks, from *Birdsong*

205 *They need praying for ....*

(When the Federal Court decision compulsorily ended segregation in the city's schools) six year-old Ruby Bridges was the sole African American student at her school, which meant that for a while she was also the only student there. For weeks she had to be escorted to school by federal marshals. One day, her teacher saw her mouthing words as she passed the lines of angry white parents hurling abuse. When the teacher reported this to Coles, he was curious: what had she said?

When he asked her, Ruby said that she had been praying for the white parents. Coles was surprised. Why was she praying for them? 'Because they needed praying for,' she answered. She had heard in church about Jesus' dying words, 'Father, forgive them, for they know not what they do', and had taken them to heart. Coles saw in Ruby Bridges and in those like her, the seeds of America's re-birth.

Johann Christoph Arnold, reporting the words of Robert Coles, a child psychiatrist,
from *The Lost Art of Forgiving*

206 *From Anger to Acceptance*

Helen Worth has been infected with the AIDS virus since 1981. A happily married woman she contracted the HIV virus through a contaminated blood transfusion in a routine operation.

She learned that she was HIV positive in 1988 after donating blood during a blood drive in her home town. She says that her students saved her life, literally, as they persuaded her to donate blood. From 1981 to 1988 doctors didn't know why she was so tired. 'I returned from vacation,' says Helen, 'and there was a letter from the American Red Cross stating that I was HIV positive'. She decided to leave teaching after the results of a survey showed that most of her colleagues and students could not cope with someone infected with the virus.

Now, having lived with the virus for 14 years, she has gone through a complete change of attitude, from anger to acceptance. She was angry when medical evidence showed that she was probably infected by a gay male. Her wrath ended dramatically. She was the only woman in a doctor's waiting room sitting with many males, most of them probably either drug addicts or gays. Her body language indicated to them that she did not want to be there. Then a young, very ill man walked in. He went over to Helen, held out his arms and said, 'Will you hug me? My mother won't talk to me ... I need a woman's arms. She stood up and grabbed him.

'That was my release,' says Helen. She describes the incident as God's way of letting her see that this disease goes far beyond all the prejudices she had built up.

Summarized from *News Share*, the magazine of the Council for World Mission

Forgive us our sins, as we forgive...

207 *Why forgive?*

It's easy for folk who live in a virtual paradise, who have enough to eat, farms, nice homes, businesses etc., to preach about forgiveness. But, is it really fair to say that to people who live in hellholes — jobless, threatened by imminent death by starvation — people who are, as Franz Fanon put it, 'the wretched of the earth'? Are they to forgive the fat, well-fed millions who voted for their starvation? Who voted for war? Who voted for prisons? Who voted for their perpetual repression? Who wish, in their heart of hearts, that they were never born? Should they forgive them for the repression to come? For the genocide that is to come?

Mumia Abu-Jamal, an African-American writer on Pennsylvania's death row,
from *The Lost Art of Forgiving*

208 *Reconciliation is not an absolute principle*

Much theology today takes 'reconciliation' as the key to the resolving of problems. On the face of it this may sound very Christian. But is it? The fallacy here is that 'reconciliation' has been made into an absolute principle that must be applied in all cases of conflict or dissension.

But not all cases of conflict are the same. We can imagine a private quarrel between two people or two groups whose differences are based upon misunderstandings. In such cases it would be appropriate to talk and negotiate in order to sort out the misunderstandings and to reconcile the two sides.

But there are other conflicts in which one side is right and one side is wrong. There are conflicts where one side is a fully armed and violent oppressor while the other side is defenceless and oppressed. There are conflicts that can only be described as the struggle between justice and injustice, good and evil, God and the devil. To speak of reconciling these two is not only a mistaken application of the Christian idea of reconciliation, it is a total betrayal of all that Christian faith has ever meant.

Nowhere in the Bible or in Christian tradition has it ever been suggested that we ought to try to reconcile good and evil, God and the devil. We are supposed to do away with evil, injustice, oppression and sin — not come to terms with it.

The Kairos Document 1985

Save us from
the time of trial

We must have no illusions:
we shall not walk on roses

Versions of the Lord's Prayer

The Good News Bible versions (British usage edition, 1976)

Our Father in heaven,
May your holy name be honoured;
may your kingdom come;
may your will be done in earth as it is in heaven.
Give us today the food we need.
Forgive us the wrongs we have done,
as we forgive the wrongs that others have done to us.
Do not bring us to hard testing,
but keep us safe from the Evil One.

Matthew 6. 9b – 13

Father:
May your holy name be honoured;
may your kingdom come.
Give us day by day the food we need.
Forgive us our sins,
for we forgive everyone who does us wrong.
And do not bring us to hard testing.

Luke 11. 2b – 4

209 Under Orders

Already in 1940 the order had gone out. Incurables and the insane were no longer to be a burden on the Reich. Three high officials descended upon the Bethel institution (a huge hospital for epileptics and the mentally ill). 'Herr Pastor,' they said, 'the Fuehrer has decided that all these people must be gassed.' Von Bodelschwingh looked at them calmly. 'You can put me in a concentration camp, if you want; that is your affair. But so long as I am free you do not touch one of my patients. I cannot change to fit the times or the wishes of the Fuehrer. I stand under orders from our Lord Jesus Christ.'

John Foster

210 My sister in Christ

It was the widespread rebellion against the central government in 1964 which was to bring persecution and death to many Congo Christians. The actions of the Simbas, or Lions, were usually predictable. 'Why did you shelter a white woman?' asked the Simba military court of one pastor. 'Because she is my sister in Christ, the child of my own heavenly Father,' was the reply. Although he was condemned to be shot, the effect of his bearing on the Simba major was such that he set him free.

T. A. Beetham

211 I am a Christian

To every question Sanctus replied in Latin: 'I am a Christian.' This he confessed again and again, instead of name and city and race and all else, and no other word did the heathen hear from his lips. When nothing else was left to inflict upon him they applied red-hot brazen plates to the most tender parts of his body. And though these were burning, Sanctus himself remained unbending and unyielding, and firm in his confession: for he was bedewed and strengthened by the heavenly fountain of the water of life which issues from the side of Christ. His poor body was a witness to what he had undergone — one whole wound and bruise, contracted, having lost the outward form of a man — in which body Christ suffered and accomplished mighty wonders, bringing the adversary to nought and showing for the example of those that remained that nothing is to be feared where the love of the Father is, nothing is painful where there is the glory of Christ...

Letter from the Christians of Lyons and Vienne, preserved in *Eusebius*

Save us from the time of trial

212 *Thascius Cyprianus*

The proconsul Galerius Maximus ordered Cyprian to be brought before him...

GM	Are you Thascius Cyprianus?
C	I am.
GM	Do you appear as the pope* of these impious men?
C	I do.
GM	The most sacred emperors have commanded you to conform to the Roman rites.
C	I refuse.
GM	Take heed for yourself.
C	Do as you are bid; in so clear a case I may not take heed.

Galerius, after briefly conferring with his judicial council, with much reluctance pronounced the following sentence, 'You have long lived an irreligious life, and have drawn together a number of men bound by an unlawful association, and professed yourself an open enemy to the gods and the religion of Rome; and the most pious, most sacred and august Emperors Valerian and Gallienus have endeavoured in vain to bring you back to conformity with their religious observances; — whereas, therefore, you have been apprehended as principal and ringleader in these infamous crimes, you shall be made an example to those whom you have wickedly associated with you; the authority of law shall be ratified in your blood.'
He then read the sentence of the court from a written tablet: 'It is the sentence of this court that Thascius Cyprianus be executed with the sword.'

C	Thanks be to God.

from the *Acta proconsularia of St. Cyprian* in *A New Eusebius*

* The title 'pope' was used of all bishops until the 5th century

213 *Expect the Desert*

We must have no illusions:
    we shall not walk on roses,
    people will not throng to hear us and applaud,
    we shall not always be aware of divine protection.
If we are to be pilgrims for justice and peace
we must expect the desert.

Helder Camara

214 *You must worship Caesar...*

Let the magistrate place on the first stand the statue of the god, Augustus, father of Caesar; on the second, to the right, that of Julia Augusta and on the third that of Tiberius Caesar, the city providing the statues for the magistrate. And in addition let him place a table in the middle of the theatre and an incense burner, and before the arrival of the artists let the members of the council and all the colleges of magistrates burn incense for the safety of the princes...

Greek inscription from AD 14–15, the beginning of the reign of Tiberius

215 *How can I?*

When the Pro-Consul pressed him and said: 'Take the oath and I let you go, revile Christ,' Polycarp said: 'Eighty and six years have I served him and he has done me no wrong: how then can I blaspheme my King who saved me?'

The final words before of 90–year-old Polycarp, Bishop of Smyrna, in his refusal to reject Christ and take the oath to the Emperor

216 *Marching Song of the Dalit* Women*

Defying police degradation
Tossing aside tradition
We have come!
Dalit, battered woman, worker, farmer,
We have come!
To end dowry, rape and abused authority;
To stop wife beating and cruelty
We have come!
To wipe out women's suppression;
To remove caste oppression;
To free humanity
In a march we have come.

Anon.

Translated from Hindi

*The Dalits are outcaste Indian people

217 A Memory

... there is a memory locked in my heart that begs to be shared.

It is the memory of a young couple — not yet in their thirties — whom I saw some months ago in a large hall that had been converted into a military courtroom, waiting for the case to be called in which they stood accused with some ninety other young people.

I had met the young man before martial law. He was a university student, a leader, brilliant, articulate, involved. That day in the courtroom he sat on a rattan chair, almost motionless, staring blankly ahead, his mouth half open, totally oblivious to the people and the chatter around him: for he had been detained under martial law, punished so repeatedly and brutally, and subjected to so large a dose of what the military call the truth serum, that his mind had cracked. He is confined, to this day, in the mental ward of a military hospital.

Behind him stood his wife, straight and proud, one hand lightly resting on the crown of his head, the other touching his shoulder, tenderly yet defiantly ready to spring on anyone who might wish to hurt her husband.

As I looked at the couple, I saw in them the face of every Filipino; and I knew that martial law could crush our bodies; it could break our minds; but it could not conquer our spirit. It may silence our voice and seal our eyes; but it cannot kill our hope and obliterate our vision. We will struggle on, no matter how long it takes or what it costs, until we establish a just community of free men and women in our land, deciding together, working and striving together, but also singing and dancing, laughing and loving together.

Jose W. Diokno, Philippines

218 *Question marks*

The question marks of history remain. Dietrich Bonhoeffer's Christian convictions brought him to resist Hitler. Yet, he dies, even as the guns outside Berlin announce that Hitler's moment of unholy glory is finally over. Was Hitler more powerful than God? Is God powerless against the South African government? And yet Steve Biko dies, naked, horribly, at the hands of those who also profess to be Christian. Martin Luther King could have given the world so much more. He taught us love, obedience, courage. And yet this apostle of love and non-violence is killed by the violence he himself refused to employ. Is God less powerful than the forces of evil? Archbishop Romero dies with the chalice of holy communion in his hands. Was God not powerful enough to stop the death of such a man? The fire rages on, the flames leaping up in their eagerness to devour. And dare we believe, and obey?

'They were bound and thrown into the burning fiery furnace.' No miracle happens. It is over. Or is it? The king springs to his feet in amazement: 'I can see four men walking freely in the heat of the fire ...' (Daniel 3.25) Here lies the wonder of it all. God does not extinguish the fire but does much more: God moves into the fiery furnace with Shadrach, Meshach and Abednego. And they discover not only the meaning of true obedience, they also discover the joy of what has been called heavenly solidarity, which follows human obedience.

For the joy of the obedient child of God lies not in the fact that the risk is eliminated or the trial set aside, so that the act of obedience would no longer be necessary. No, it lies in the discovery that this God will suffer with you.

Alan Boesak, from *Walking on Thorns*

219 *Emmanuel*

At a difficult and trying time I received a call from one of the members of our congregation. 'It may not mean much,' she said, 'but I wanted to let you know that we are praying for you. Don't give up the struggle for what is right and just.' Then she gave me a text from Psalm 91 to remember: 'Because he cleaves to me in love I will deliver him; I will protect him because he knows my name ...' As I stood there, feeling the strength and joy of such love, my eyes became blurred but my vision cleared, and I understood what it meant to have God with me in the fiery furnace.

Alan Boesak, from *Walking on Thorns*

220 *Nada te turbe*

Let nothing disturb you;
let nothing dismay you;
all things pass:
God never changes.
Patience attains
all it strives for.
He who has God
finds he lacks nothing:
God alone suffices.

Teresa of Avila, 1515 – 1582

221 *In Place of a Curse*

At the next vacancy for God, if I am elected,
I shall forgive last the delicately wounded
Who, having been slugged no harder than anyone else,
never got up again, neither to fight back,
nor to finger their jaws in painful admiration.

Those who are wholly broken, and those in whom
mercy is understanding, I shall embrace at once
and lead to pillows in heaven. But those who are
the meek by trade, baiting the best of their betters
with the extortions of a mock-helplessness
I shall take last to love, and never wholly.

Let them all into Heaven — I shall abolish Hell —
but let it be read over them as they enter:
'Beware the calculations of the meek, who gambled nothing,
gave nothing, and could never receive enough.'

Source unknown

222 *The Clay Speaks*

Just a handful of earth
in the beginning
lifted from inertia
then mixed with the water of life.

At first formless, resisting,
yet gradually moulded and reshaped
as slowly I learned to relinquish
my former existence;

then painfully pressed and recreated
in places so thin I thought I would break
not knowing the ultimate purpose.

Worse was to come — the terrible fire
the searing unspeakable heat.
How could I possibly know
the transforming fire
would change my being so completely?

Then slowly as the flames died
I began to understand
though still not fully.

Remaining dull of colour
yet different
hardened for what is to come
I sensed the desire for colour —
a glazing beauty of shining radiance;

so even knowing the furnace —
how can I pray to be spared
another firing?

Cecily Taylor

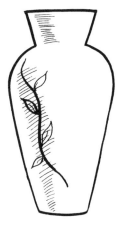

223 *The Pounding of the Rice*

How much the rice must suffer
under the pestle;
But, after the pounding,
it comes out
white like cotton.

The same thing often happens
to people in this world.
Misfortune's workshop
turns them
to polished jade.

Ho Chi Minh, Vietnam

224 *Firewood*

If it is you that I want
what you ask
is that I become
as driftwood
washed up
upon your shore
to be
    bleached by the sun
    pounded by the surf
    scoured by the sand
until I,
hollowed hallowed
dry and brittle
am ready
for the spark
    which ignites
for the fire
    which consumes
for the smoke
    which sanctifies.

I burn fiercely
leaving only
ash
warm sand
and the taste of salt.

Craig Steeland

225 *Stand Fast*

But if you live the time
that no man will give you good counsel,
nor no man will give you good example;
when you shall see virtue punished
and vice rewarded;
if you will then stand fast
and firmly stick to God,
upon pain of my life,
though you be but half good,
God will allow you for the whole good.

Thomas More 16th Century

226 *Persecutor and Persecuted*

O Lord, I beseech you,
make me thankful for the grace you have given me.
As for those who persecute me,
in the name of religion,
thinking they are doing your will,
pardon them in your mercy.
For if you had revealed to them
what you have revealed to me,
they would not be acting as they are.
And if you had hidden from me
what you have hidden from them,
I might have been the persecutor instead of the persecuted.
Glory to you in all you do.
Glory to you in all you will.

Al-Hallaj Al-Mansure

227 *No matter what persecution?*

I have not suffered.
Not yet anyway.

I stubbed my toe once
And it nearly bled.
I knocked my thumb with a hammer
Turning it blue.
I remember being in hospital
Ten long days.
But I cannot say I've suffered.

I've been depressed
Longing for tomorrow's sunshine.
I've been disappointed
And had to change my life's direction.
I've carried burdens
Even for a second mile
But I cannot say I've suffered.

At school some laughed
At the church-going boy.
In the laboratory
They thought it odd
To study science
And believe in God.
It pushed me to the side
But I cannot say I suffered.

I made a promise once.
They asked me:
    'Do you promise to maintain the truth of the gospel
    whatever trouble or persecution may arise?'*
And I said, 'Yes'
And they ordained me.
Though I'm not sure what the question meant.

You see,
I've never suffered.
Not yet anyway.

Anon

** Part of the ordination/induction liturgy of the United Reformed and other
Churches*

Deliver us from evil

When we stumble, hold us;
When we fall, lift us up;
When we are hard pressed with evil, deliver us;
When we turn from what is good, turn us back.

Versions of the Lord's Prayer

The Church of England Alternative Service Book (ASB) version (1980)

Our Father in heaven,
hallowed be your name,
your kingdom come,
your will be done on earth as in heaven.
Give us today our daily bread.
Forgive us our sins
as we forgive those who sin against us.
Lead us not into temptation
but deliver us from evil.
For the kingdom, the power and the glory are yours
now and for ever. Amen

228 *Remember us, Lord*

Remember us all, Lord, for good.
Have pity on us all, be reconciled with us all.
Fill our storehouses;
Preserve our marriages, nurture our children;
Lead forward our youth, sustain our old;
Comfort the weak-hearted, gather the scattered;
Restore the wanderers, and unite them to your Church.
Set free the troubled;
Voyage with the voyagers, travel with the travellers;
Protect the widow, shield the orphan;
Rescue the captive, heal the sick.
Remember, O Lord, all those who are on trial,
In exile, or in whatever affliction,
And remember all those who need your great mercy.
Remember those who love us, and those who hate us;
Remember those who through ignorance and forgetfulness
We have not mentioned.
Pour out your rich pity and save all your people, O Lord.

Lancelot Andrewes, 1555–1626

229 *A Prayer for Grace*

I will lift up my hands to your commandments,
The commandments I have loved.
Open my eyes that I may see;
Incline my heart that I may desire;
Order my steps that I may follow
The way of your commandments.
O Lord God, be my God,
You alone, no one else, nothing else, beside you.
May I worship you and serve you
In truth of spirit, in reverence of body,
In blessing of lips.

Lancelot Andrewes, 1555–1626

230 *Prayer before Birth*

When I am born,
Let not machines destroy me,
Let not fires
Shrivel up my skin,
Let me not be blind
Deaf or dumb,
I am small and harmless
Same as others.

When I am born
Let reproduction be complete
So I may carry on your world.
If I die
Use my body
To save others
So they may carry on your world

When I am born,
I am asking God
Not just for myself
But for others as well
When we are in need
Please provide for us.
Keep us from harm
From the terrible things
We must face.

Jannette Clay

231 *Before Abraham was*

Eternal God,
before we were born,
you were there,
working in the womb,
letting life be.

Before we could speak for ourselves,
you were there,
leading us with love,
washing us with grace.

Before we could decide for ourselves,
you welcomed us to your knee
and took us to your heart.

When we had only just believed,
you had already forgiven us.
Before we could keep to the law,
you had pronounced us innocent
and called us just.

And then, when we went to war,
you had already won the battle for life.
When hope seemed lost and our security in danger,
we remembered our home with you.

Now we look forward to a new peace
and find again that you are there before us.
Before Abraham was, and before all time,
you are God, the great 'I am.'

Michael Durber

232 *I am afraid of the dying*

His is the life
that is bread
broken, piece by piece,
for all people.

His is the love
that is wine
poured, drop by drop,
for our thirst.

Day by day
we are baptised
into his hard self-dying.

Day by day
we are offered life or death
life through death.

Day by day
we are drawn
into the beckoning fire
that purifies,
transfigures,
inspires,
and yields us again:
Light into the world.

Julie M. Hulme

233 *The Undefeated*

A vigil for those persecuted for their religious beliefs

We keep this silent watch of night
    in simple prayer
and not with any special light
    to help us there,

yet trust that in our lowly way
    the pleas we make
may rise upon the break of day
    for others' sake:

the valiant ones who struggle on
    with searing need,
whose hope is held by faith hard won —
    the hidden seed.

Margaret Connor

234 *We laid our suffering before God*

Some Catholics, including Fr. Amyot invited me to join them in prayer. Seven or eight of us gathered, secretly of course, in the shed used as a lavatory. In prayer we laid before God our suffering, our rags, our filth, our fatigue, our exposure, our hunger, and our misery

Aimé Boniface, Holocaust survivor, later a French Reformed pastor

Deliver us from evil

235 The road to agnosticism

When I was about nine I asked God to eliminate my brother Gordon. Painlessly but irreversibly. At Lindisfarne, as it happens, to which we had been taken not to reflect upon the Viking raids of which mother had probably never heard but to walk out to the island along the causeway and have a picnic thereon. And Gordon and I raced across that spit of land, and Gordon being one year older and quite a bit faster was all set to win, of course. And I gasped up this prayer, in fury and passion, meaning it — oh, quite meaning it. Never again, I said, will I ask You for anything. Anything at all. Just grant this. Now. Instantly. It is interesting to note that I had to demand Gordon's extinction, not that I be made a faster runner. And of course God did nothing of the kind and I sulked throughout a glorious windswept sea-smelling afternoon and became an agnostic.

Source unknown

236 An alternative kind of power

We are afraid, we turn away from genuine obedience, we succumb to the pressures and intimidation of the powerful because God does not seem to strike down our executioners. The fiery furnace keeps threatening. Does that mean that God is weak? Is God weak because the divine response is not commensurate with human expectation?

God does not respond to Nebuchadnezzar in terms of Nebuchadnezzar's power. True. But then God's power is a totally different kind of power. God's 'weakness' is not the powerlessness which is the opposite of power; it is an alternative kind of power. It is not weakness but *strength* that enables God to become one with us, even in our suffering and pain, and through being present to deliver us. To have a powerful God is wonderful, and our God is powerful. But to have a powerful God who 'emptied himself, taking the form of a servant ... and became obedient unto death, even death on a cross' (Philippians 2. 6–8) — that is grace and power for us.

Alan Boesak, from *Walking on Thorns*

237 *Temptation*

The billows swell, the winds are high,
Clouds overcast my wintry sky;
Out of the depths to Thee I call, —
My fears are great, my strength is small.

O Lord, the pilot's part perform,
And guard and guide me through the storm;
Defend me from each threatening ill,
Control the waves, — say, 'Peace! be still.'

Amidst the roaring of the sea
My soul still hangs her hope on Thee;
Thy constant love, thy faithful care,
Is all that saves me from despair.

Dangers of every shape and name
Attend the followers of the Lamb,
Who leave the world's deceitful shore,
And leave it to return no more.

Though tempest toss'd and half a wreck,
My Saviour through the storms I seek;
Let neither wind nor stormy main
Force back my shatter'd bark again.

William Cowper, 1731 – 1800
from *The Olney Hymns*

Deliver us from evil

238 *Memorial Service*

For those fallen in battle

Why shouldn't we be asked
to pray for enemy dead
as well as ours?

The flowers of our remembrance
do not discriminate;
those petals drop their blood
on wood or stone
where watery autumn sunlight
filters through
as once it did on muddied fields.

Whatever accident decreed his side,
whatever verdict
passing years decide,
a dead man is a dead man
anywhere
and someone mourns him — here
— or there.

Margaret Connor

239 *Dedication*

One day
I would like to take
Both my hands
   (For I consider life itself
   too dear to lose)
Dip them in petrol
Then set them alight
With a candle flame
And dedicate them
To those who acted
While I wept and wrote.

Mahmood Jamal, Pakistan

No Empty Phrases

240 *God alone is Lord of the conscience*

We have to trust God, and not human beings, when it comes to matters of deepest importance in human life.

The weakness of all brands of Fundamentalism is fully exposed at this point. Fundamentalism has a false understanding of God taken from Dispensationalism. According to the Dispensationalist view, the Holy Spirit was around to inspire people only during the Apostolic Age. After that the Spirit lay on its deathbed until the canon was closed about 400 C.E. But, according to this view, the Spirit is not sufficiently present today to lead people to faith, to guide interpretation of Scriptures, to help believers make decisions, to direct the Churches in the paths they should go, to illumine the minds of students. No, not the Spirit of God, but 'Big Brother' must tell us what to do. To quote the now well-known words of Adrian Rogers, then President of the Southern Baptist Convention: 'If we (I'm not sure whether this meant 'we Southern Baptists' or 'I, your pope') decide that pickles have souls, then those who teach in our seminaries ought to teach that pickles have souls or they ought not to take our money.'

Here we are listening to the *corporation mentality* which has taken control of Neo-Fundamentalism thinking, as it has shifted from the principle of separation to the principle of control, in order to effect its goals. That is the very same mentality that developed during the high Middle Ages and came to its most graphic expression in the Bull *Unam Sanctam* of Pope Boniface VIII: 'It is absolutely necessary for salvation for every human creature to be subject to the Roman pontiff.' The other side of that conviction is Ignatius Loyola's Rule 23 for Thinking with the Church: 'To arrive at the truth in all things, we ought always to be ready to believe that which seems to us white is black, if the hierarchical Church so defines it.'

For European Christians today the question is: Is this the model that will bring hope to European Christianity, or is it a model which will invite disaster?

E. Glenn Hinson, from *Theology Themes* of the Northern Baptist College

Deliver us from evil

241 *To hear — and not to hear*

He read from the scroll of the prophet Isaiah
there, in the synagogue at Nazareth,
words that had been heard
and not heard,
for six hundred years.
And once again as he read the familiar passage
they heard
and did not hear.

He has sent me to announce good news to the poor,
to proclaim release for prisoners
and recovery of sight for the blind.

They were poor, clinging to their poverty;
prisoners, seeking no release;
blind, lacking the desire to see.

There is an illusion of comfort and peace
in standing outside the battle;
to be liberated,
to follow his way
could be dangerous;
the synagogue might rise against them,
they might find themselves
being hurried to a stoning
or a cross.

To let the broken victims go free,
to proclaim the year of the Lord's favour.

For those waiting with closed minds
this was too little,
altogether too little.
He had rolled up the scroll
without finishing the passage;
as though the Lord's favour
was for any
and everybody
without thought of race, or creed,
or past record.

Edmund Banyard

242 *Bold cowards*

We have grown brave, we modern folk,
Eager to kiss the moon's reluctant face,
Defying every harness, chain and yoke,
Kicking our rockets down the field of space.
We flout established customs undismayed,
Leap time and space with buttons we have pressed,
Attempt to outwit death at his own trade,
Transplanting hearts from dead to living chest.

And yet we are afraid to step aside
From lockstepped columns marching without aim,
To sit alone in silence, stripped of pride,
Refocusing our thoughts on wisdom's flame,
To climb that stony path few feet have trod
Where sacrifice and faith discover God.

Muriel Hammond

243 *Do not be afraid*

Are you afraid
    in the night of pitch darkness?

Are you frightened
    by the raging billows?

Are you fearful
    of calamities life brings?

Do not be afraid!
The Lord is coming!

The Lord will turn
Everything harmful into
Everything edifying.

C. M. Kao

From *Testimonies of Faith, Letters and Poems from Prison in Taiwan*

244 *The Blessing of Light*

May the blessing of Light be on you —
Light without and light within;

May the light of the sun shine on you —
Warming you with a fire of gold;

May the light of the moon caress you —
Calming your mind in a sleep of dreams;

May the light of the stars shine on you —
Lifting your heart to thoughts beyond;

May the light in your soul speak gently —
Guiding your feet in the ways of love;

May the blessing of Light be on you —
Light without and light within.

Cecily Taylor

245 *At last to your glory!*

O Lord our God,
Who has called us to serve you,
In the midst of the world's affairs,
When we stumble, hold us;
When we fall, lift us up;
When we are hard pressed with evil, deliver us;
When we turn from what is good, turn us back;
And bring us at last to your glory.

Alcuin, 4th century

246 *Until the light came*

Until the light came
I did not realize
that I had become so accustomed
to existing in darkness.

Until the light came
I did not realize
how much rubbish
I had accumulated about me.

Until the light came
I did not realize
how small the dwelling
in which I had confined myself.

At first it was dazzling, penetrating.
It wasn't easy to adjust to the light.
Too many things stood revealed
I'd rather not have seen.
Yet gradually,
and with fresh and startling clarity,
new hopes, new joys, new life
stood revealed,
waiting for me to grasp them —
if I would!

But I did not have to face such decisions —
until the light came.

Edmund Banyard

Deliver us from evil

247 *Let your light shine on me*

As the sun rises, Lord,
Let your light shine on me.
Destroy the darkness about me,
Scatter the darkness before me,
Disperse the darkness behind me,
Dispel the darkness within me.
Let your light shine on me.

As the sun rises, Lord,
Let your light shine on me.
The warmth of your Presence,
The brightness of your love,
The radiance of your joy,
The shining of your hope.
Let your light shine on me

As the sun rises, Lord,
Let your light shine on me.
Your light to guide,
Your light to lead,
Your light to direct,
Your light to brighten.
Let your light shine on me.

David Adam

248 *Lord, seek us*

O Lord seek us, O Lord find us
In Thy patient care,
Be thy love before, behind us,
Round us everywhere.
Lest the god of this world blind us,
Lest he forge a chain to bind us,
Lest he speak us fair,
Turn not from us, call to mind us,
Find, embrace us, hear,
Be Thy love before, behind us,
Round us everywhere.

Christina Rossetti

249 We beg you, Lord,
to help and defend us.

Deliver the oppressed,
pity the insignificant,
raise the fallen,
show yourself to the needy,
heal the sick,
bring back your people
    who have gone astray,
feed the hungry,
lift up the weak,
take off the prisoner's chains,

May every nation come to know
that you are God,
that Jesus Christ is your Child
that we are your people,
the sheep of your pasture.

Clement of Rome, c. 200

No Empty Phrases

The kingdom, the power and the glory

How wondrous great, how glorious bright
Must our Creator be,
Who dwells amidst the dazzling light
Of vast infinity!

Versions of the Lord's Prayer

The Revised English Bible versions(1989)

The Revised English Bible is a revision of the New English Bible (1961)

Our Father in heaven,
may your name be hallowed;
your kingdom come,
your will be done
on earth as in heaven.
Give us today our daily bread.
Forgive us the wrong we have done,
as we have forgiven those who have wronged us.
And do not put us to the test,
but save us from the evil one.

Matthew 6. 9b – 13

Father, may your name be hallowed;
your kingdom come.
Give us each day our daily bread.
And forgive us our sins;
for we too forgive all who have done us wrong.
And do not put us to the test.

Luke 11. 2b – 4

250 *The Power is Love*

Not with a roll of drums
nor trumpet's blare
but clothed in silence comes
Love down the stair.

After the flames' quick roar,
the whirlwind storm,
with still and stronger core
Love fills our form.

Then in the noise and spin
of our small days,
quiet amid the din
Love moulds our ways.

Margaret Connor

251 *Five kinds of power*

There are five kinds of power: the exploitative, the competitive, the manipulative, the integrative, and the nurturing.

Exploitation, competition, and manipulation are powers used to destroy. Exploitative power is 'power over' another. Competitive power is 'power against' another. Manipulative power is 'under the counter' power used dishonestly — though perhaps legally — to 'persuade' another.

Nurturing and integrative powers are those which build up instead of undermining others: they are gentle, freeing, and caring. They are the only hope for our times.

Based on the comments of the psychologist Rollo May

252 *Not what we think*

no fiery deluge,
no fist clenching rapture,
no star-strewn apocalypse.

only
a
woman
labouring,
only
the needy cry
of
a
child
in the dark.

Glory is not what you think.

Source unknown

253 *Wonder*

A God and yet a man?
A maid and yet a mother?
Wit wonders how wit can
Conceive this or the other.

God, Truth itself, doth teach it.
Man's wit sinks too far under
By reason's power to reach it:
Believe and leave to wonder.

Anon, 15th century

254 *God of Washing*

God of washing, God of unmade beds,
God of dented saucepans and worn-out brooms,
your presence in the most ordinary things
often takes me by surprise.

I listen to the morning news
and think of your presence
at a United Nations' peace conference,
at the launching of a space probe,
or in the development of a vaccine,
or the discovery of a new planet.
Then I look down and see you
winking in bubbles of detergent.

God of washing,
God of stains and missing buttons,
wherever else you might be,
you are right here with me,
defrosting and cleaning the freezer,
picking up bits of plastic toys
from the living room floor,
and each time you nudge my heart
with the warmth of your presence,
recognition leaps like a song.

I know it! Oh, I know it!

God of washing,
God of vacuum cleaner bags,
God of sparrows, lilies and mustard seeds,
my house is your tabernacle.

Joy Cowley
from *Psalms Down-Under* (Catholic Supplies [N.Z.] Ltd.)

255 *The Divine Glory*

How wondrous great, how glorious bright
    Must our Creator be,
Who dwells amidst the dazzling light
    Of vast infinity!

Our soaring spirits upward rise
    Toward the celestial throne,
Fain would we see the blessed Three,
    And the almighty One.

Our reason stretches all its wings,
    And climbs above the skies;
But still how far beneath thy feet
    Our grovelling reason lies!

Lord, here we bend our humble souls,
    And awfully adore,
For the weak pinions of our mind
    Can stretch a thought no more.

Thy glories infinitely rise
    Above our labouring tongue;
In vain the highest seraph tries
    To form an equal song.

In humble notes our faith adores
    The great mysterious King,
While angels strain their nobler powers,
    And sweep the immortal string.

Isaac Watts

256 *Paradox*

Strange paradox of faith —
    it fluctuates
yet at its very core
    perpetuates

itself — so if we try
    to struggle free
the more enmeshed we know
    ourselves to be,

but in the course of this
    our hidden fight
may find that we are drawn
    nearer the light.

Did Thomas really have
    to test his ground?
He praised but did he touch?
    In our profound

relief that nothing need
    our hope destroy,
we come in silence yet
    shouting for joy.

Margaret Connor

257 *All redeemed*

The Lord's ascension also marks the glorification
    of the universe.
The universe rejoices, money rejoices, power rejoices,
    all material things —
    farms and estates — everything
rejoices because the day will come when the Supreme Judge
    will redeem from sin, from slavery, from shame,
all that God has created
    and that human beings are using for sin,
    for an affront against their fellows.
The redemption is already decreed,
    and in his power God has raised up Christ our Lord.
Christ has gone up to heaven as a witness to final justice.

Oscar Romero

258

O Thou who art veiled in the shrouds of thy glory,
so that no eye can perceive thee!
O Thou who shinest forth in the perfection of thy splendour,
so that the hearts of mystics have realised thy majesty!
How shalt though be hidden,
seeing that thou art for ever present,
and watchest over us.

Ibn 'Ata' Allah of Alexandria, 14th century

259 *The glory of God within us*

Our deepest fear is not that we are inadequate.
Our deepest fear is that we are powerful beyond measure.
It is our light, not our darkness, that frightens us.
Who am I to be brilliant, gorgeous, talented and fabulous?
Actually, who are you not to be?
You are a child of God,
Your playing small doesn't serve the world.
There is nothing enlightened about shrinking
so that other people won't feel insecure around you.
We are born to make manifest the glory of God within us.
It is not just some of us, it's in everyone.
And as we let our own light shine, we unconsciously
give other people permission to do the same,
so we are liberated from our own fear,
our presence automatically liberates others.

Nelson Mandela
from the 1994 Inaugural Speech

260 *Glory be to God*

Glory be to God for dappled things —
    For skies of couple-colour as a brinded cow;
       For rose-moles all in stipple upon trout that swim;
Fresh-firecoal chestnut falls; finches wings;
    Landscape plotted and pieced — fold, fallow, and plough;
       And all trades, their gear and tackle and trim.

All things counter, original, spare, strange;
    Whatever is fickle, freckled (who knows how?)
With swift, slow; sweet, sour; adazzle, dim;
He fathers-forth whose beauty is past change:
    Praise him.

Gerard Manley Hopkins

261 *High Flight*

An airman's ecstasy

Oh, I have slipped the surly bonds of earth
And danced the skies on laughter-silvered wings;
Sunward I've climbed and joined the tumbling mirth
Of sun-split clouds — and done a hundred things
You have not dreamed of; wheeled and soared and swung
High in the sun-lit silence. Hovering there
I've chased the shouting wind along, and flung
My eager craft through footless halls of air;
Up, up the long delirious burning blue
I've topped the wind-swept heights with easy grace,
Where never lark nor even eagle flew;
And while, with silent lifting mind I've trod
The high untrespassed sanctity of space,
Put out my hand, and touched the face of God.

John Gillespie Magee

262 *Helleborus Niger*

The Christmas rose
never flowers at Christmas
unless you cushion it with care,
hype-up its promise,
and bed it down with close-strewn hay
as in a manger.
Its pristine glory comes much later:
March or April; Easter-time,
and so belies its name.

And so it was
that only later;
after the messy stable and the bloody cross,
by resurrection hindsight
we beheld his glory.

Donald Hilton

263 Tuesday September 14th 1915

...the dug-outs have been nearly blown in, the wire entanglements are a wreck, and in among (this) chaos of twisted iron and splintered timber and shapeless earth are the fleshless, blackened bones of simple men who poured out their red, sweet wine of youth unknowing, for nothing more tangible than Honour or their Country's Glory or another's Lust of Power. Let him who thinks that war is a golden glorious thing, who loves to roll forth stirring words of exhortation, invoking Honour and Praise and Valour and Love of Country with as thoughtless and fervid a faith as inspired the priests of Baal to call on their slumbering deity, let him look at a little pile of sodden grey rags that cover half a skull and a shin bone and what might have been its ribs, or at this skeleton lying on its side, resting half-crouching as it fell, supported on one arm, perfect but that it is headless, and with the tattered clothing still draped around it; and let him realise how grand & glorious a thing it is to have distilled all Youth and Joy and Life into a foetid heap of hideous putrescence. Who is there who has known and seen who can say that Victory is worth the death of even one of these?

Vera Brittain, from War Diaries 1913–1917

264 Anthem for Doomed Youth

What passing-bells for these who die as cattle?
    Only the monstrous anger of the guns.
    Only the stuttering rifles' rapid rattle
Can patter out their hasty orisons.
No mockeries now for them; no prayers nor bells,
    Nor any voice of mourning save the choirs, —
The shrill demented choirs of wailing shells;
    And bugles calling for them from sad shires.

What candles may be held to speed them all?
    Not in the hands of boys, but in their eyes
Shall shine the holy glimmers of good-byes.
    The pallor of girl's brows shall be their pall;
Their flowers the tenderness of patient minds,
And each slow dusk a drawing down of blinds.

Wilfred Owen

The kingdom, the power and the glory

265 *People are so clever*

We are the clever ones
With big heads and skilful hands
Reaching for power and glory.
To make them ours.

Yet, are we bright enough
To storm your kingdom
By the unaided power of our intellects?
Or even to realise
It can't be done that way?

Forgive us for our monkey cleverness.
Grant that it finds
Its proper resting place.

Is the ditch
One of your mansions, Lord?

W. S. Beattie

266 *Everyone Sang*

Everyone suddenly burst out singing;
And I was filled with such delight
As prisoned birds must find in freedom,
Winging wildly across the white
Orchards and dark-green fields; on — on — and out of sight.

Everyone's voice was suddenly lifted;
And beauty came like setting sun:
My heart was shaken with tears; and horror
Drifted away... O, but Everyone
Was a bird; and the song was wordless; the singing will be done.

Siegfried Sassoon
April 1919

267 *Kingdom, power, and glory*

'Kingdom' is not a ruling
autocrat upon the throne,
scattering orders like cheap confetti
and destined to lie discarded on the ground.
> A kingdom is a relationship
> of love,
> and joyful obedience;
> responsibility shared,
> each subject truly valued.
The kingdom is yours, eternal Christ.

'Power' is not oppression;
with victims meekly bowing,
or fleeing for their lives.
> Power is foot-washing,
> love enabling love,
> talents released
> and new life reaching upwards.
The power is yours, eternal Christ.

'Glory' is not flamboyant show,
jewels sparkling,
processions of majesty and pomp,
marble halls and kneeling multitudes.
> Glory is a child laid low in manger,
> a listening teacher and a shy healer,
> a criminal's cross and borrowed grave
> and an unproved resurrection
> built alone on questing faith.
The glory is yours, eternal Christ.

From all time and for ever, here and in every place:
The kingdom, the power and the glory are yours, eternal Christ.

Donald Hilton

No Empty Phrases

Now and for ever

There is but one freedom,
to put oneself right with death.
After that, everything is possible.

The end is a beginning

The Christian promise

Mourning, crying ... and hope

Time and beyond

Versions of the Lord's Prayer

The New Revised Standard Version versions (1989)

The New Revised Standard Version is a revision of the Revised Standard Version (1952);,itself based on the American Standard Version (1901) which was a variant of the (British) Revised Version (1884) but embodying the preferences of the American scholars associated with the work.

Our Father in heaven,
    hallowed be your name.
    Your kingdom come.
    Your will be done
        on earth as it is in heaven.
    Give us this day our daily bread.
    And forgive us our debts,
        as we have forgiven our debtors.
    And do not bring us to the time of trial,
        but rescue us from the evil one.

Matthew 6. 9b – 13

Father, hallowed be your name.
    Your kingdom come.
    Give us each day our daily bread.
    And forgive us our sins;
        for we ourselves forgive everyone indebted to us.
    And do not bring us to the time of trial.

Luke 11. 2b – 4

268 *The Hidden*

Everything has its roots in God.
In the greening of the tree,
the music of falling water,
the surge of the incoming tide,
the rise and fall of seaweed,
the barking of seals on a rock,
the dive of the humpback whale,
the I AM is manifest.

Everything is contained in God.
In the smoke from a driftwood fire,
the wind sharpening leaves of a flax,
the shadow of trout in a moonlit stream,
the first fall of snow on the mountain,
the kingfisher flying to her nest,
the I AM is moving.

Everything speaks of God.
In the winner's shout of celebration,
the laughter round the dinner table,
the child's cry of pain in the night,
the groan of the woman in childbirth,
the sigh of the man's last breath,
the I AM is heard.

God is everything's secret.

Joy Cowley
From *Psalms Down-Under* (Catholic Supplies [N.Z.] Ltd.)

The end is a beginning

269 *Lazarus*

I don't intend it to happen.
It just sneaks up on me
and before I know it
there's been a kind of death,
part of me wrapped in a shroud
and buried in a tomb
while the rest of me stands by
wondering why the light has gone out.
Then you, my Friend, all knowing,
seek me out and knock
at the edge of my heart,
calling me to come forth.
I argue that I can't.
Death is death and I'm too far gone
for story book miracles.
But you keep on calling,
'Come forth! Come forth!'
and the darkness is pierced
by a shaft of light
as the stone begins to move.

My Friend,
I don't know how you do it
but the tomb has become
as bright as day, as bright as love,
and life has returned.

Look at me!
I'm running out
dropping bandages all over the place.

Joy Cowley
from *Psalms Down-Under* (Catholic Supplies [N.Z.] Ltd.)

270 Brought to life

Jean Vanier: 'I begin to discover something: that this wounded person looks at me, approaches me — all this does something to me, the wounded person calls me forth ... we are brought to life by the eyes and hands of wounded people who seem to call us forth to life.'

On a dusty road,
an outcast, with both hands outstretched,
offered me a blessing.
And deep within, a child who felt cast out —
unrecognised, oppressed —
found a voice, and made a song.

In a shanty town,
one who was in rags, both hands outstretched,
offered me a gift.
And, deep within, a hungry, naked child —
felt fed and richly clad.

In a hospital,
one who will die tomorrow, hands outstretched,
offered me a healing.
And, deep within, a child who hurt and bled —
and felt disordered and diseased —
was held, and helped to dance.

> There is a touching place
> where those whose wounds are seen
> reach out to hidden wounds
> behind facades of affluence, well-being,
> confidence; and say,
> 'I recognise you: we are one.'

> And some will turn away, afraid
> to be unmasked.
> And some will weep, at once appalled and glad
> to be so recognised; and free
> to receive at last and to be heard;
> enabled thus to hear and share,
> within the commonwealth of woundedness,
> the strange, unsettling glory of new life.

Kate Compston

271 *Fear no more*

Fear no more the heat o' the sun,
    Nor the furious winter's rages;
Thou thy worldly task is done,
    Home art gone, and ta'en thy wages.
Golden lads and girls all must,
As chimney-sweepers, come to dust.

Fear no more the frown o' the great,
    Thou art past the tyrant's stroke;
Care no more to clothe and eat,
    To thee the reed is as the oak.
The sceptre, learning, physic must
All follow this, and come to dust.

Fear no more the lightning-flash,
    Nor the all-dreaded thunder-stone;
Fear not slander, censure rash;
    Thou hast finished joy and moan.
All lovers young, all lovers must
Consign to thee, and come to dust.

No exorciser harm thee!
Nor no witchcraft charm thee!
Ghost unlaid forbear thee!
Nothing ill come near thee!
Quiet consummation have;
And renownèd be thy grave.

William Shakespeare

272 *Worse than death itself*

We had long thought of death, of being executed during our long period in solitary confinement. But suddenly confronting a gun being pointed at us seemed to break up the ice barrier that had prevented us talking to one another of our fear of death. We were in agreement about one thing, and perhaps it was a romantic notion, but we were both convinced that if it ever came to it, then we would ask to have one last look at the sun before the sentence was carried out. On reflection neither of us seemed frightened of the real possibility of this. So long sunk in contemplation of our own death, we had come to terms with it and dismissed it. But we both shared a sense of the ultimate indignity of being executed in a strange building within four enclosed walls. That would be worse than death itself.

The floodgate began to open. We eased ourselves out of our quiet and unspoken apprehension of one another. We began slowly, carefully but honestly to tell one another of the things we felt, the things we thought about, and our experiences during that time alone.

It is always difficult for two people to come together and talk openly about those experiences that might normally be termed religious. But once we had begun and realized that each was listening to the other, there was no need to hold back.

Brian Keenan speaking of his imprisonment alongside John McCarthy

273 *Accepting death*

There is but one freedom,
    to put oneself right with death.
After that, everything is possible.
    I cannot force you
to believe in God.
    Believing in God amounts to
coming to terms with death.
    When you have accepted death,
the problem of God will be solved —
    and not the reverse.

Albert Camus

274 *Holy Sonnet*

Death be not proud, though some have called thee
Mighty and dreadful, for thou art not so;
For those whom thou think'st thou dost overthrow
Die not, poor death, nor yet canst thou kill me.
From rest and sleep, which but thy pictures be,
Much pleasure, then from thee much more must flow;
And soonest our best men with thee do go,
Rest of their bones, and souls' delivery.
Thou art slave to Fate, chance, kings and desperate men,
And dost with poison, war, and sickness dwell,
And poppy or charms can make us sleep as well,
And better than thy stroke; why swell'st thou then?
One short sleep past, we wake eternally,
And death shall be no more, Death thou shalt die.

John Donne

275 *Go forth upon thy journey*

Go forth upon thy journey, Christian soul!
Go from this world! Go, in the Name of God
The Omnipotent Father, Who created thee!
Go, in the Name of Jesus Christ, our Lord,
Son of the living God, Who bled for thee!
Go, in the Name of the Holy Spirit, who
Hath been poured out on thee! Go, in the name
Of Angels and Archangels; in the name
Of Thrones and Dominations; in the name
Of Princedoms and of Powers; and in the name
Of Cherubim and Seraphim, go forth!
Go, in the name of Patriarchs and Prophets;
And of Apostles and Evangelists.
Of Martyrs and Confessors, in the name
Of holy Monks and Hermits; in the name
Of holy Virgins; and all Saints of God,
Both men and women, go! Go on thy course;
And may thy place be found in peace,
And may thy dwelling be the Holy Mount
of Sion: — through the Same, through Christ our Lord.

John Henry Newman
from *The Dream of Gerontius*

276 *All my Answers*

I pulled my sack of question marks
right up the stairs of heaven
and shook them out
all clattering
before the feet of God.
He smiled that I had carried them
for such a weary distance
and I could smile
because it seemed
I would not need them now —

for all my answers floated up
like rainbow bubbles laughing
and children ran to catch them
down the lanes of Paradise.

We threw the dots for distant stars
and then we gently gathered
two armfuls of
some brand new moons
that nobody had used.
We fixed a question hook in each
and on these silver hangers
the people hung
their coats of care
they would not need them now —

for all their answers floated up
like rainbow bubbles laughing
and children ran to catch them
down the lanes of Paradise.

Cecily Taylor

277 *Being Dead Already*

Being dead already
I had no need of the fear
That had constricted me
Like a winding shroud.

I wondered at first
Why I felt so free
Then realised I had forgotten it
And left it behind in the grave.

'Couldn't I go back and tell them
They won't need their fear either?'
I suggested.
'That's just what I *did*,'
He said.

Cecily Taylor

278 *Healing forgiveness*

Looking down into my father's
dead face
for the last time
my mother said without
tears, without smiles
but with *civility*,
'Good night, Willie Lee, I'll see you
in the morning.'
And it was then I knew the healing
of all our wounds
is forgiveness
that permits a promise
of our return
at the end.

Alice Walker

279 *This passing world; this eternal love*

The present form of the world passes away,
and there remains only the joy of having used this world
    to establish God's rule here.
All pomp, all triumphs, all selfish capitalism,
    all the false successes of life will pass
    with the world's form.
All of that passes away.
What does not pass away is love.
When one had turned money, property, work in one's calling
    into service of others,
then the joy of serving
    and the feeling that all are one's family
does not pass away.
In the evening of life you will be judged on love

Oscar Romero

*The above was part of the homily Romero gave at the funeral service of a priest
— and four young men — who had been killed by the security forces whilst leading a spiritual retreat for a Catholic youth group*

280 *Bede's Sparrow*

'Such,' he said, 'O King, seems to me the present life of men on earth, in comparison with that time which to us is uncertain, as if when on a winter's night you sit feasting with your ealdormen and thegns, — a single sparrow should fly swiftly into the hall, and coming in at one door, instantly fly out through another. In that time which it is indoors it is indeed not touched by the fury of the winter, but yet, this smallest space of calmness being passed almost in a flash, from winter going into winter again, it is lost to your eyes. Somewhat like this appears the life of man; but of what follows or what went before, we are utterly ignorant.

The Venerable Bede (673–735)
From *Ecclesiastical History of the English People*

281 My faith in You is nothing but
the dark path in the night
between the abandoned shack
of my poor, dim, earthly life
and the brilliance of your Eternity

Karl Rahner

282 *The world is not my home*

For my own part, I am transported with impatience to join the society of my departed friends, and to be with the mighty men of the past of whom I have heard. To this glorious assembly I am quickly advancing; and if some divinity should offer me life over again I would reject the offer. This world is a place Nature never designed for my permanent abode; and I look upon my departure, not as being driven from my home, but as leaving my inn.

Cicero

283 *Cloud of Witnesses*

What if time is not a continuous line,
But a series of concentric circles?
Then human life would not be,
As for Bede's sparrow, a matter of
Flying into the light for a brief period
On a long migration from darkness to
Darkness. More like an appearance
In a vast arena, where all the actors
Play their part under brilliant lights,
Then fade into the auditorium, beyond the glare,
Making space for new arrivals.
We laugh and love, and struggle to make sense of
Half a script, finding the writing
Difficult to read, frustrated in our effort
By the inability of others
To get their lines right, or their sheer
Obstructiveness; ad-libbing our way
Out of difficult situations,
Rejoicing when all goes well.
And all around us, those who
Have had their turn, or
Wait in trepidation for their cue,
Watch, supporting us with sympathetic
Tears or laughter, urging us on
In loving fellowship.
Then, when the play is over,
And the lights go up,
We shall meet them, and have time,
Or will it be eternity, to enjoy
Their company. Time too to meet the Author,
And discuss our part, learning the value of
Our contribution, which had never been in doubt
In his mind, only in our faltering confidence.

Ann Lewin

Now and for ever

284 Take a building

God shall have a starring role in my history of the world. How could it be otherwise? If He exists, then he is responsible for the whole marvellous appalling narrative. If He does not, then the very proposition that He might has killed more people and exercised more minds than anything else. He dominates the stage. In His name have been devised the rack, the thumbscrew, the Iron Maiden, the stake; for Him have people been crucified, flayed alive, fried, boiled, flattened; He has generated Crusades, the pogroms, the Inquisition and more wars than I can number. But for Him there would not be The St. Matthew Passion, the works of Michelangelo and Chartres Cathedral.

So how am I to present Him — this invisible all pervasive catalyst? How am I to suggest to my reader (no informed enlightened reader — a visitor from outer space, let us say) the extraordinary fact that for much of recorded time most people have been prepared to believe in the presidency over all things of an indefinable unassuageable Power?

I shall take a building. A building shaped like a cross, furnished neither for habitation nor defence. I shall multiply this building by a thousand, by ten thousand, by a hundred thousand. It may be as small as a single room; it may soar into the sky. It may be old or it may be new; it may be plain or it may be rich; it may be of stone or it may be of wood or it may be of brick or of mud. This building is in the heart of cities and in deserts and upon mountains. It is in Provence and Suffolk and Tuscany and Alsace and in Vermont and Bolivia and the Lebanon. The walls and the furnishings of this building tell stories; they talk of kings and queens and angels and devils; they instruct and they threaten. They are intended to uplift and to terrify. They are an argument made manifest.

The argument is another matter. What I am trying to demonstrate at this point is the amazing legacy of God — or the possibility of God — by way not of ideas but of manipulations of the landscape. Churches have always seemed to me almost irrefutable evidence. They make me wonder if — just possibly — I might be wrong.

Which is how I came once to pray. To kneel down in St. George's Pro-Cathedral, Cairo and ask a putative God for forgiveness and help. I was thirty-one.

Source unknown

The Christian Promise

285 *And the trumpets sounded*

Then Mr Honest called for his friends, and said unto them, 'I die, but shall make no will. As for my honesty, it shall go with me; let him that comes after be told of this.' When the day that he was to be gone, was come, he addressed himself to go over the River. Now the River at that time overflowed the banks in some places. But Mr Honest in his life-time had spoken to one Good-conscience to meet him there, the which he also did, and lent him his hand, and so helped him over. The last words of Mr Honest were, 'Grace reigns.' So he left the world.

After this it was noised abroad that Mr. Valiant-for-Truth was taken with a summons, by the same Post as the other; and had this for a token that the summons was true, *That his pitcher was broken at the fountain.* When he understood it, he called for his friends, and told them of it. Then said he, 'I am going to my fathers, and though with great difficulty I am got hither, yet now I do not repent me of all the trouble I have been at to arrive where I am. My sword, I give to him that shall succeed me in my pilgrimage, and my courage and skill, to him that can get it. My marks and scars I carry with me, to be a witness for me that I have fought his battles who now will be my rewarder.' When the day that he must go hence was come many accompanied him to the River side, into which, as he went, he said, *'Death, where is thy sting?'* And as he went down deeper, he said, *'Grave where is thy victory?'* So he passed over, and the trumpets sounded for him on the other side.

John Bunyan
From *The Pilgrim's Progress*

Now and for ever

286 *To imitate the passion of my God*

For my part, I am writing to all the churches and assuring them that I am truly in earnest abut dying for God — if only you yourselves put no obstacles in the way. I must implore you to do me so much untimely kindness; pray leave me to be a meal for the beasts, ˙or it is they who can provide my way to God.

All the ends of the earth, all the kingdoms of the world would be of no profit to me: so far as I am concerned, to die in Jesus Christ is better than to be monarch of earth's widest bounds. He who died for us is all I seek: he who rose again for us is all I desire. Suffer me to attain to light, light pure and undefiled; for only when I am come thither shall I be truly a man. Leave me to imitate the passion of my God. If any of you has God within himself, let that man understand my longings, and feel for me, because he will know the forces by which I am constrained.

Ignatius, from *The Letter to the Romans*

287 Grant, O Lord,
that we may live in Thy fear,
die in Thy favour,
rest in Thy peace,
rise in Thy power,
reign in Thy glory;
for the sake of Thy Son,
Jesus Christ our Lord.

William Laud, 1573–1645

No Empty Phrases

288 *I Am*

I am — yet what I am none cares or knows,
My friends forsake me like a memory lost;
I am the self-consumer of my woes,
They rise and vanish in oblivious host
Like shades in love and death's oblivion lost,
And yet I am — and live, with shadows tossed

Into the nothingness of scorn and noise,
Into the living sea of waking dreams,
While there is neither sense of life nor joys,
But the vast shipwreck of my life's esteems;
And e'en the dearest, that I loved the best,
Are strange — nay, rather stranger than the rest.

I long for scenes where man has never trod,
A place where woman never smiled or wept,
There to abide with my creator, God,
And sleep as I in childhood sweetly slept,
Untroubling and untroubled where I lie;
The grass below — above the vaulted sky.

John Clare

289 *Resurrection and judgement*

In faith we expect God to complete his purpose for all mankind and for each individual person by endowing men beyond their death with new resources for being alive unto God in fellowship with Jesus Christ. In the powers already granted through the gift of the Holy Spirit, Christians have a foretaste of this new being. It has, for its indispensable grounds, the judgement of God through which men will know at last the whole truth about themselves, and the saving love of God which removes all condemnation from those joined in manhood with his obedient Son their Saviour Jesus Christ. For those who trust the grace of the Lord Jesus Christ the judgement of God's holy love is the gateway to his everlasting mercy.

from *A Declaration of Faith*
The Congregational Church in England and Wales (1967)

Now and for ever

290 *Palast Hotel, Berlin W, 15 December 1901: Programme of the Second Symphony by Gustav Mahler*

We are standing by the coffin of a man beloved. For the last time his life, his battles, his sufferings and his purpose pass before the mind's eye. And now, at this solemn and deeply stirring moment, when we are released from the paltry distractions of everyday life, our hearts are gripped by a voice of awe-inspiring solemnity, which we seldom or never hear above the deafening traffic of mundane affairs. What next? it says. What is life — and what is death? Have we any continuing existence?

Is it all an empty dream, or has this life of ours, and our death, a meaning? If we are to go on living, we must answer this question.

The next three movements are conceived as intermezzi.

Second Movement. Andante

A blissful moment in his life and a mournful memory of youth and lost innocence.

Third Movement. Scherzo

The Spirit of unbelief and negation has taken possession of him. Looking into the turmoil of appearances, he loses together with the clear eyes of childhood the sure foothold which love alone gives. He despairs of himself and of God. The world and life become a witch's brew; disgust of existence in every form strikes him with an iron fist and drives him to an outburst of despair.

Fourth Movement. The primal dawn. (Alto solo)

The moving voice of ingenuous belief sounds in our ears. 'I am from God and will return to God! God will give me a candle to light me to the bliss of eternal life.'

Fifth Movement

We are confronted once more by terrifying questions. A voice is heard crying aloud: the end of all living beings is come — the Last Judgement is at hand and the horror of the day of days has come.

The earth quakes, the graves burst open, the dead arise and stream on in endless procession. The great and the little ones of the earth — kings and beggars, righteous and godless — all press on — the cry for mercy and forgiveness strikes fearfully on our ears. The wailing rises higher — our senses desert us, consciousness dies at the approach of the eternal spirit.

The Last Trump

is heard — the trumpets of the Apocalypse ring out; in the eerie silence that follows we can just catch the distant, barely audible song of a nightingale, a last tremulous echo of earthly life! A chorus of saints and heavenly beings softly breaks forth:

No Empty Phrases

'Thou shalt arise, surely thou shalt arise.' Then appears the glory of God! A wondrous, soft light permeates us to the heart — all is holy calm!

And behold — it is no judgement — there are no sinners, no just. None is great, none is small. There is no punishment and no reward.
An overwhelming love lightens our being. We know and are.

From *Gustav Mahler, Memoirs and Letters* by **Alma Mahler**

291 *Blessed Assurance*

Death may dissolve my body now,
    And bear my spirit home:
Why do my minutes move so slow,
    Nor my salvation come?

With heavenly weapons I have fought
    The battles of the Lord,
Finish'd my course, and kept the faith,
    And wait the sure reward.

God has laid up in heaven for me
    A crown which cannot fade;
The righteous Judge at that great day
    Shall place it on my head.

Nor hath the King of grace decreed
    This prize for me alone;
But all that love, and long to see
    The appearance of his Son.

Jesus, the Lord, shall guard me safe
    From every ill design;
And to his heavenly kingdom take
    This feeble soul of mine.

God is my everlasting aid,
    And hell shall rage in vain;
To him be highest glory paid,
    And endless praise, Amen

Isaac Watts

Now and for ever

292 *A Vision of Heaven*

Bring us, O Lord God, at the last awakening
into the house and gate of heaven,
to enter into that gate and dwell in that house,
where there shall be no darkness nor dazzling,
but one equal light;
no noise nor silence,
but one equal music;
no fears nor hopes,
but an equal possession;
no ends nor beginnings,
but one eternity,
in the habitations of thy majesty and thy glory,
world without end.

John Donne, 1571–1631

293 *And that will be heaven*

and that will be heaven

and that will be heaven
at last   the first unclouded
seeing

    to stand like the sunflower
turned full face to the sun   drenched
in light   in the still centre
held   while the circling planets
hum with utter joy
                seeing and knowing
at last   in every particle
seen and known   and not turning
away
        never turning away
again

Evangeline Paterson

Mourning, crying, anger
... and hope

294 Gifts

For Michael, bereaved of his daughter

I wanted to bring you a mantle of comfort.
You said: I am not cold, and the coat
is stifling me.

I wanted to bring you a plateful of wisdom.
You said: I am not hungry, and besides
you forgot the knife and fork.

I wanted to bring you a reservoir of peace.
You said: Time enough to drink the still waters:
death is very quiet.

Only when I brought you my own desolation,
my storm of tears and raging, did you say:
Now you are talking — I accept your gift.

Kate Compston

295 *Remember*

Remember me when I am gone away,
　　Gone far away into the silent land;
　　When you can no more hold me by the hand,
Nor I half turn to go yet turning stay.
Remember me when no more day by day
　　You tell me of our future that you planned:
　　Only remember me; you understand
It will be late to counsel then or pray.
Yet if you should forget me for a while
　　And afterwards remember, do not grieve:
　　For if the darkness and corruption leave
　　A vestige of the thoughts that once I had,
Better by far you should forget and smile
　　Than that you should remember and be sad.

Christina Rossetti

296 *I am not there*

Do not stand at my grave and weep —
I am not there, I do not sleep.
　　I am a thousand winds that blow,
　　I am the diamond glint on snow,
　　I am the sunlight on ripened grain,
　　I am the gentle autumn rain.
　　When you awaken in the morning's hush
　　I am the swift up-lifting rush
　　Of quiet birds in circled flight.
　　I am the soft stars that shine at night.
Do not stand at my grave and cry —
I am not there, I did not die.

Anon

297 *Widow's Beads*

With trembling touch I take up
the thin thread of life alone
and string each day's lack-lustre beads
together one by one.
My fumbling fingers moving aimlessly,
connect a baubled band
without design, or colour scheme,
the careless craft of heedless hands.
So through the days,
the weeks, the months, the years,
time's necklace grows.
Dull browns and greys
depict the cheerless days,
pale pastels show where hope creeps in,
through kindly friend or kin;
the brighter hues,
a sudden unexpected splash
of scarlet, green, or blue,
highlight the times
when new life stirs in me.
Then I can turn the golden key
that opens memory's lock,
and meekly learn to hold
in humble hand that other shining strand
of peerless pearls
that were our treasured days together,
so your love around me curls
its dear unchanging warmth.
Then fortified, my heart the lesson heeds,
and I begin again, with surer touch,
to thread my widow's beads

Kath Crane

298 *Surrounded by a cloud of witnesses*

Each occasion
we glimpse them:
that turn of a head
that smile
the way she walked
his sense of humour,
each time
a knife turns
in our heart.

In time,
through the windows of our tears
we see them
and smile.
In time
we let go of sorrow.
In time
beauty and music,
remembered places
bring solace not pain.
In your time
God of all time
may what we have sown in pain
be reaped in joy.

Kate McIlhagga

299 *Dona nobis pacem*

Be merciful, be gracious; spare him, Lord.
Be merciful, be gracious; Lord, deliver him
    From the sins that are past;
       From Thy frown and Thine ire;
           From the perils of dying;
           From any complying
           With sin, or denying
           His God, or relying
  On self, at the last;
    From the nethermost fire;
From all that is evil
From the power of the devil;
Thy servant deliver,
For once and for ever.
By Thy birth and by Thy Cross
Rescue him from endless loss;
By Thy death and burial,
save him from a final fall;
By Thy rising from the tomb,
    By Thy mounting up above,
    By the Spirit's gracious love,
Save him in the day of doom.

John Henry Newman
from *The Dream of Gerontius*

300 *Be present with us* (Luke 24. 13–35)

Be present with us, Journeying God,
as we walk the road from the graveyard.
Share our dismay at the ways of the world,
shoulder our burden of grief for what could have been,
and then, with your eyes aflame,
urge us, convict us, inspire us with your words of truth
and hope beyond hope.

Stay with us, Befriender God,
as a guest in our homes.
Break bread, pour wine, call down a blessing,
and then, when we reach out to hold you,
go before us through the night to the troubled city,
carrying joy.

Julie M Hulme

301 *Toward eternity*

Because I could not stop for Death,
He kindly stopped for me;
The carriage held but just ourselves
And Immortality.

We slowly drove, he knew no haste,
And I had put away
My labor, and my leisure too,
For his civility.

We passed the school where children played
At wrestling in a ring;
We passed the fields of gazing grain,
We passed the setting sun.

We paused before a house that seemed
A swelling of the ground;
The roof was scarcely visible,
The cornice but a mound.

Since then 'tis centuries; but each
Feels shorter than the day
I first surmised the horses' heads
Were towards eternity.

Emily Dickinson

302 *All that is left?*

I remember stooping down and picking up something black near the (concentration camp) crematorium. I realised it was a bone. I was going to throw it down again and I thought, 'My God, this may be all that is left of someone.' So I wrapped it up and carried it with me. A couple of days later, I dug it out of my pocket and buried it.

George Kaiser
an American soldier in the army of liberation, Germany, 1945

303 *Death by Degrees*

They hail me as one living,
　But they don't know
That I have died of late years,
　Untombed although?

I am but a shape that stands here,
　A pulseless mould,
A pale past picture, screening
　Ashes gone cold.

Not at a minute's warning,
　Not in a loud hour,
For me ceased Time's enchantments
　In hall and bower.

There was no tragic transit,
　No catch of breath,
When silent seasons inched me
　On to this death...

A Troubadour-youth I rambled
　With Life for lyre
The beats of being raging
　In me like fire

Thomas Hardy

But when I practised eyeing
The goal of men,
It iced me, and I perished
A little then.

When passed my friend, my kinsfolk,
Through the Last Door,
And left me standing bleakly,
I died yet more;

And when my Love's heart kindled
In hate of me,
Wherefore I knew not, died I
One more degree.

And if when I died fully
I cannot say,
And changed into the corpse-thing
I am today;

Yet is it that, though whiling
The time somehow
In walking, talking, smiling,
I live not now.

304 Evil vanquished; creation glorified

God's wisdom, love and power will be fully vindicated in the triumph of his purposes for the universe and for the corporate life of mankind within it. This triumph is presented in the Bible as the outcome of a final conquest by God of all evil powers which at present bring human life into the blindness and bondage and rebellion of sin. Our minds cannot bring into focus this aspect of God's dominion; but we are encouraged to believe that the long struggle for right in which mankind shares will have a satisfying outcome when God brings his sovereignty to a triumphant completion.

We look forward to acts of God which bring a final transformation to human life and admit human beings to share in his own eternal joy and felicity. Creatures have been called into being to reflect the unimaginable glory of the everlasting God. Cleansed from sin we shall see God in Jesus Christ in open splendour, and he will make us like himself. We do not know in what universal framework human lives so transfigured will be set; nor how in that framework God's other purposes for his created universe will be fulfilled. We do know that God is the source, the guide, the goal of all that is, and that in his serenity he sees the end from the beginning. He lives in the blessedness of everlasting joy and peace, and his creatures will share in that blessedness and rejoice in it.

The Congregational Church in England and Wales,
from *A Declaration of Faith* 1967

305 Be with me

'Be with me' I whispered, as the sun began to rise
'I am here' He answered, 'I am by your side'.

'Be with me' I whispered, 'when I have your work to do'
'I am here' He answered, 'I am here with you.'

'Be   with   me'   I   whispered,   'for   I   sometimes   feel   alone'
'I am here' He answered, 'you are never on you own.'

'Be with me' I whispered, 'when I have a load to bear'
'I am here' He answered, 'I am always there.'

'Be with me' I whispered, 'when I feel I have to grieve'
'I am here' He answered, 'I will never leave.'

'Be with me' I whispered, 'may we never part'
'I am here' He answered, 'I am dwelling in your heart. '

Claire Seal

306 *Hallowed ground*

Silent the bell, it tolls no more,
The Church is just a shell, closed is the door,
Closed by people with common sense,
cold indifference, lack of pence,
A lone silhouette on a bleak Pennine top.
Do they ever pause and stop
to think of the Church in its prime,
Christmas, Easter, and Harvest time?
Often have I climbed those meadows steep
when winter snow lay white, deep,
to sing my praise of Saviour's birth,
'Good will to all, peace on earth.'
The lark soars high his song to sing,
to welcome yet another Spring.
The soft wind whispers in the grass,
of another hill, another cross.
Beneath granite, stone and earthen mound,
deep within that hallowed ground,
lie Father, Mother, Sister, Friend,
What to them this modern trend?
Have we betrayed their loving trust,
will there again blossom from the dust
a brave new Church proudly planned?
If not, I pray they will understand.

Anon

307 Problem

We've got a problem, Lord:
We're getting older.
As a fellowship
We're dying on our feet.

There must be something we can do.
Let's think, think very hard,
Pool all our bright ideas and draw up plans,
Set targets and define priorities.
Now, let's get weaving.
And, Lord,
Bless what we choose to do,
To prove we are your servants.

Only, one thing —
It seems so simple
That I hardly like to mention it,
But — when did we ask you, Lord,
Just what you wanted?

Do we not dare to ask?
Or do we not believe
That you will answer?
Or would we rather not commit ourselves
In case you did?

W. S. Beattie

308 *The Unchanging Message*

Dusk falls on the village chapel,
No evening service,
Not for many a year,
People are too busy,
Many distractions.
Has the church failed?
    Overloaded itself,
    Too many committees,
    Over organised,
    Outmoded forms of worship?

Yet the Gospel message is unchanged,
Still as powerful today
As when the Lord called:
'Follow me!'

Y Mochyn Daear

309 *Signs of the Kingdom in our own community*

We need to ask, surely, where are the signs of the Kingdom in our own community? Where are the values of the Kingdom being lived out — not just talked about or written about? ... We find that a difficult and even threatening question. Bishop Stephen Verney recounts how he set himself the task of sitting down with every church council in the diocese and asking each one: 'What is God doing here and now?' Some people told him it was an improper, even indecent, question. 'You can't expect God to be here — not *now*...' That seldom lasted. 'Slowly, after time for reflection, people began to share amazing insights of grace at work in individuals, groups, whole communities ... It was clear that for many it was the first time they had thought of it that way ... and what a joyful discovery it was for them! Perhaps, after all, God was alive and living amongst them.'

Charles Elliott
From *Praying the Kingdom*

Now and for ever

310

We began this day with God
We end this day with God.
Tomorrow, and tomorrow
we will know his presence
is with us in all we do.
We go out into the world
with God

From Asia

The daughter of Karl Marx once confessed to a friend that she had never been brought up in any religion and had never been religious. 'But' she said, 'the other day I came across a beautiful prayer which I very much wish could be true'.

'And what was that prayer?' she was asked. Slowly the daughter of Karl Marx began repeating in German:

'Our Father who art in heaven...'

Robert Latham

No Empty Phrases

Copyright acknowledgements

The compiler and publishers express gratitude to the authors and copyright holders who have allowed their material to be used in this anthology. Every effort has been made to trace copyright owners but if any rights have been inadvertently overlooked , or where copyright searches have proved unfruitful, they would welcome information to correct errors or omissions. Any corrections will gladly be made in subsequent editions. Copyright permissions are listed in item order. Where more than one item derives from the same copyright source, numbers for later items are indicated in brackets after the first entry.

Item	Copyright
1	(2, 4) Source unknown
3	(8, 91,191, 217, 239) © indicated authors. Taken from *Your Will Be Done* (1984), The Christian Conference of Asia. Used by permission.
5	© Jim Cotter. From *Prayer at Night's Approaching,* Cairns Publications, 1997. Also (6, 11) © Jim Cotter. Used by permission.
7	(50, 61, 66, 96, 136, 154, 165, 166, 173, 183, 202, 262, 267) © Donald Hilton.
10	(30, 32, 41,141, 171, 172, 177, 265, 307) © W. S. Beattie. Used by permission
12	(47, 159, 270, 294) © Kate Compston. Used by permission.
15	© Paul Bunday. Permission sought.
16	© Lady Helena McKinnon. Used by permission.
17	© Kathy Galloway, from *Love Burning Deep: Poems and Lyrics,* SPCK, 1993.
18	(23, 51, 62, 65, 152, 254, 268, 269) © Joy Cowley. From *Psalms Down-Under,* Catholic Supplies (N.Z.) Ltd, 80 Adelaide Road, Wellington, New Zealand. e-mail: catholic.supplies@clear.net.nz. Used by permission.
20	Used by author's permission. © 1996 Hope Publishing. Administered by Copycare, PO Box 77, Hailsham BN27 3EF, United Kingdom. Used by permission.
21	© Ecumenical Review, World Council of Churches. From *Ecology and the Recycling of Christianity.*
22	(189) © Joy Cowley. From *Aotearoa Psalms,* Catholic Supplies (N.Z.). Address and e-mail as at item 18.
24	(131, 150, 241) © Edmund Banyard. From *Turn but a Stone,* NCEC. Used by permission.
27	(34, 42,53, 68, 72, 89, 102, 112, 193, 233, 238, 250, 256) © Margaret Connor. Used by permission.
28	(74, 247) © David Adam. From *Power Lines,* SPCK, 1992. Used by permission.
29	(98, 289, 304) From *A Declaration of Faith,* the Congregational Church in England & Wales, 1967. © The United Reformed Church. Used by permission.

Copyright acknowledgements

86   From *Long Walk to Freedom* by Nelson Mandela. Published by Little Brown and Co. UK. Used by permission.

88   Translation © by H. J. Richards.

90   © Publishing Dept, Visva-Bharati University, Calcutta. Used by permission.

95   © Roger McGough. Reprinted by permission of The Peters Fraser and Dunlop Group Limited in behalf of Roger McGough.

97   Taken from *An Anthology for the Church Year*, published by Kevin Mayhew Ltd, Buxhall, Stowmarket, Suffolk IP14 3DJ, and used by permission of the publishers.

100   (125, 181) © Colin Ferguson. Used by permission.

103   © Robert Winnett. Permission sought.

104   (130) From Epworth Review September 1992 (19:3) © 1992 Epworth Press. Used by permission of Methodist Publishing House.

105   © Tibor Tollas and Livia Var. Permission sought.

106   © Stainer & Bell 1987. Used by permission.

107   © Cecily Taylor. From *Contact* published by Galliard. Used by permission of author.

109   © Stainer & Bell. Used by permission.

113   From *Mere Christianity*. Published by HarperCollins. Used by permission.

114   Publisher unknown.

115   © Cecily Taylor. Used by permission.

117   (120) © Browne Barr. Permission sought.

118   © Joan Brockelsby. Permission sought.

119   © Marc Heslop. Used by permission of The Christian Education Movement.

121   Publisher unknown.

124   © Times Newspapers Limited 1998. From The Times of 27 March 1998.

127   Publisher unknown.

132   © Felicity Prescott. Permission sought.

134   © Derek Mahon. From *Poems 1962–1978*. Permission sought from Gallery Press, County Meath, Ireland.

138   © Peter Brice White Cottage, Front Street, Worstead, North Walsham, Norfolk, NR28 9RW.

139   From *Sophie's World* by Jostein Gaarder. Used by permission of The Orion Publishing Group.

Copyright acknowledgements

146   © Tim Woods. Source unknown.

147   © Churches of Christ, Malawi. Permission sought.

148   (169) © Cecily Taylor. First published in Envoi. Used by permission.

153   From *Hymn to Matter*. Publisher unknown.

155   © John Campbell. South Aston United Reformed Church, Birmingham, UK, B6 5ET.

156   Source unknown

157   Source unknown

158   Source unknown

160   © June Plaice. Used by permission.

162   © World Council of Churches. Taken from *Compassionate and Free.* Used by permission.

163   Source unknown.

164   © Timothy Gorringe. From *The Sign of Love*. Published by SPCK. Used by permission of the author.

168   © Tim Presswood. From *Theology Themes* produced by the Northern Baptist College. Used by permission.

174   © Andrew M. Rudd. Permission sought.

179   (180, 184) © Kenneth Wadsworth. Used by permission.

190   © Asian Women's Resource Centre. Taken from Volume 14, No. 4 1995 of *In God's Image*. Used by permission

194   © Frank McCourt. From *Angela's Ashes*. Published by HarperCollins Publishers Ltd. Used by permission.

196   Taken from *Contours* Volume 7. No.2 June 1995. Used by permission.

197   © Michael D Goulder. Used by permission.

201   (205, 207) Quoted from *The Lost Art of Forgiving* by Johann Christoph Arnold and used by permission of The Plough Publishing House.

203   Source unknown.

204   © Sebastian Faulks. Taken from *Birdsong*. Permission sought.

206   Summarized from *Newshare,* the magazine of the Council for World Mission. Used by permission.

208   © Institute of Contextual Theology, Braamfontein, South Africa. Used by permission.

209   From *What are the Churches Doing*. Publisher unknown.

210   From *Christianity and the New Africa*. Publisher unknown.

Copyright acknowledgements

Copyright acknowledgements

Index of authors

Index of authors

Index of authors

Index of authors

Index of titles

Where an item has no title, the first line — or a significant part of it — is given.

Index of titles

Index of titles

Index of titles

Index of titles

Index of themes

This index is not exhaustive. It is given in order to increase the accessibility of the anthology by indicating how various items can be used to explore important themes frequently used in Christian education and worship. In some instances the inclusion of an item under a particular theme may go beyond the intention of the original author. It is certain that the compiler has omitted items from subjects and themes in this index which those who use the anthology will be able to add to create a more complete index. By recalling particular words, the index should also help to find items which have been used previously.

Index of themes

Index of themes

Index of themes

Index of themes

S

Sabbath	121
Sacrifice	242
Scapegoat	61
Sea-change	76
Search	26, 36, 109
Sight	46, 84
Self-centredness	180, 184
Senses	46, 84, 120, 270
Serpent	167
Service	84. 93, 94, 96, 127, 279
Shame	201, 239
Sin	167, 180, 202
Singapore	67
Socialism	127, 139, 191
Solidarity	117, 166, 218, 219
Sparrow	280, 283
Spirituality	152, 23, 26, 28, 30, 35
	36, 39, 40, 41, 46, 53
	74, 137, 138, 254, 266, 287
Spring	64
Suffering	16, 28, 65, 85, 91
	144, 227, 234, 290, 298
Sunday	23, 120, 121
Superstore	28
Sympathy	111, 117, 120, 206, 219

T

Taafe, Connor & Louise	124
Tears	296, 298
Third Reich	209
Thomas	180, 181, 256
Time	280, 281, 282
Today	108
Tolerance	138

Torrance, Thomas	137
Torture	59, 211, 216, 217
Touch	120, 170, 270
Touching place	270
Tourism	196
Town	28, 72
Transformation	62, 65, 113, 156, 203
	222–224, 232, 246, 257, 304
Treachery	61, 85
Trials	209–227, 232
Trinity	135, 255

U

Uncertainty	288
Unexpected, the	28, 31, 83, 112
	115, 128, 197, 254
Unity	17, 145, 146

V

Valiant-for-Truth, Mr	285
Virgin Birth	51
Vision	106, 122, 127, 128, 132
	134, 136, 139, 141, 147
	151, 154, 176, 189, 292

W

War	111, 190, 193, 207
	208, 234, 263, 264
Washing	254
Widow	297
Wise Men	54, 55
Wonder	43–46, 118, 128, 253
Work	110
Worship	31, 32, 38, 41, 42, 67
Worth, Helen	206
Written by children	1, 119, 128